THE REPAIR SHOP

THE REPAIR SHOP

A make do and mend guide to caring for the things you love

Foreword by **JAY BLADES**

BBC
BOOKS

CONTENTS

FOREWORD

BY JAY BLADES

'Everybody has something that means too much to be thrown away. That's where we come in.'

In the modern era it has too often been a case of 'Out with the old, in with the new.' As life moves fast, so do broken objects in this throwaway society – directly to recycling centres – as it seems easier to toss them out rather than resurrect or rejuvenate them. The days of tinkering with things that are failing or fractured are long gone.

People are daunted, probably feeling that they don't have the necessary know-how these days as old-style crafts, once handed down the generations, are being lost for the sake of hectic diaries and cheap retail.

That's where The Repair Shop comes in, with its resident experts ready and willing to take on the heavy lifting.

Behind the closed doors of The Repair Shop the rapid pace of today's living is forgotten as conservators and restorers become absorbed in their tasks, happy to spend hours and days questing for a flawless outcome on a single item.

Furniture restorer William Kirk calls it 'the workshop of dreams,' and not just because people who visit see hoped-for transformations in well-loved belongings. He and the rest of the experts are also living the dream, fixing a vast range of artefacts that might not otherwise come to their work benches.

As soon as their eyes lock on to a new project, their minds start racing about how best to achieve the right results. It turns out their single-minded attentiveness and nimble fingers are spellbinding for viewers, who are gripped by techniques and tips.

And the tale behind each item is just as compelling as the conservation or restoration process. Every story takes us at *The Repair Shop* on a sentimental journey so engrossing we forget the presence of nearby cameras and crew as it unfolds.

Critically, the team aren't refurbishing antique investments so the owners can cash in, but are putting a piece of family history back into place, priceless in a different way and making an emotional return rather than a financial one.

Although they are all masters at their chosen skill, everyone is keen to consult and collaborate on projects, to embrace new or adapted methods that will work with old items. Every day is an education and, as I tell them, if you aren't learning anything, well, what are you doing? You may as well be pushing up the daisies.

This book is designed for people who don't have years of experience behind them like *The Repair Shop* experts, but might share some of the same goals: to retrieve objects from dusty boxes, restore them to a former glory and safeguard them as a legacy to pass on to future generations. For those who want to step off the treadmill for a moment and spend a few hours of tranquillity with some much-loved ancestral item, this is the handbook that can make it happen.

Jay

INTRODUCTION

In our youth we take evidence of the quirky and the classical parked on the landing or lining the shelves very much for granted. But by degrees we lose sight of an aged desk that we knew from childhood, and the worn chair that once stood plush and proud by the door.

Computers have usurped typewriters, which themselves replaced fountain pens and the writing slopes that used to accompany them. Gramophones, radios and even jukeboxes have surrendered to mobile phones. Metal and wooden toys have long since made way for plastic counterparts. Clocks have gone digital.

It's impossible to halt progress and no one wants to stop innovation. But while shiny, modern objects churned out in distant factories by the thousand have their place in today's homes, they don't command the same deep-seated affection as something once cradled by a grandparent, evoking as that does a misty memory of childhood. Years later those once familiar items provide a bridge between generations now gone and those still unborn, who will one day inherit this family's mantelpiece treasure.

Happily, we are a nation of hoarders. Rather than ditching chipped china, perforated pictures or stopped clocks, we tend to stash them in our lofts, with every good intention to one day bring those articles that mean so much back to their former glory.

Inside the open doors of The Repair Shop the air is filled with a symphony of hammering, drilling and the clatter of tools. Here's where experts with those bygone talents in crafts and conservation have gathered to fix neglected heirlooms so that they might be saved for future generations.

There's rarely an idle moment as exceptional craftspeople pore over items that haven't been at their best for decades. Their aim is not to spruce up an object so it gets the best price at auction, as no monetary value can be put upon the sentimental journey that the sight, sound or smell of a cherished possession will induce. Everyone's focus is to get it back in pride of place in a family home. It's a place where nostalgia never gets old.

Between them The Repair Shop experts took widower Albert Thompson on a poignant trip down memory lane when they repaired his GEC portable transistor radio, bought for 50 shillings, when he was aged just 22, with his wife-to-be Eileen in the fifties. Afterwards, the radio went everywhere with them before it became a fixture of family life. When it stopped working for the first time, a repairer replaced the faulty buttons with the rounded ends of toothbrushes. This time it stopped on the second anniversary of Eileen's death — and the problems were far more technical. Nonetheless, Albert insisted he didn't want to discard the radio, despite a range of replacements now available, but needed it back in his greenhouse for peace of mind. After spending some time locating what turned out to be several major faults, radio expert Mark Stuckey sorted out the circuitry. Suzie Fletcher fitted a new handle around the old one, Jay Blades helped her clean the case while Steve Fletcher made a new dial from a clear plastic lid, a spare brass component and the bottom of a lamp stand. Albert returned to hear music beaming from the radio, the soft serenade at a pitch evocating all the best memories of his life and love.

Other items brought into The Repair Shop have a role to play in international history as well as being a pivotal part of a family story. Natalie Cummings brought along a violin in pieces, bearing a crude repair on one shoulder. The instrument had belong to an aunt, Rosa Levinsky who took it with her when she left her home in Leeds in the mid-thirties after she was invited to play in the Berlin Philharmonic. However, Russian-born Rosa was soon swept up in the turmoil of the times. As a Jew, she was first sent to Mauthausen concentration, then to Auschwitz. She spent the rest of the Second World War in the notorious death camp as part of the women's orchestra, playing to entertain guards and to distract doomed arrivals. Although orchestra members like herself escaped the gas chambers she was nonetheless kept short of food and clothing.

The emotional stress must have been phenomenal. Finally, when hostilities ceased, she returned home to Yorkshire and died in 1947. The violin went to her brother Sydney, Natalie's father, also a musician. But it had been stored in the loft for years; the finger board was detached and without strings.

Violin restorer John Dilworth eased the front face of the violin off to find a signature and a date for its manufacture: it was made in 1883 in Dresden, Germany. His approach was so considered he even included the unsightly repair that was almost certainly done at Auschwitz.

There are no challenges that aren't embraced by a team that relishes the old, the unusual and the downright obscure. It takes hours spent at the workbench to accrue the kind of experience that can breathe life into something that is at best tired, at worst entirely wrecked. Crucial among the considerations facing the team are how age and authenticity will be retained. Each expert uses tools and techniques tried and tested throughout their career.

Although much of what they accomplish is the preserve of the professionals, they also provide an antidote to today's throwaway society. The experts are keen to take the mystique out of basic care and considered restoration, to help retain as much of our social history as possible in the best order. That's where this book comes in, as it contains the combined wisdom of *The Repair Shop* experts across all their specialities. Find out how to clean, carry, care for and repair the articles that mean most to you, to safeguard your sentimental legacy for generations to come.

Conservation or Restoration?

When leather expert and saddlemaker Suzie Fletcher was confronted by a decrepit leather patterned pouffe she drew up a detailed plan for its repair. Each tessellated piece was unpicked, numbered, dabbed with saddle soap, lined with fine pig skin and sewn back together again.

The original thread was rotten and was discreetly renewed. New piping was included on the top and 300 hand stitched seams later, with the pouffe standing at twice its previous height, it was ready for return. But although the majority of the 113 decorative pieces were saved, some sections of the Egyptian pouffe were beyond repair and needed replacing. While new thread went unseen, each bit of modern leather would stand out from its age-weathered neighbour. Yet it's unlikely previously used leather taken from a 'donor' item which might have blended would have added the necessary durability.

It's a dilemma that faces master craftspeople like Suzie and the rest of The Repair Shop team on a daily basis.

There's a natural tension between conservation – preserving an item for future generations – and restoration, giving it a sense of newness. On this occasion Suzie opted to include new leather that was instantly apparent, something she felt was an honest repair that gave life to otherwise defunct furniture.

With every artefact that comes through the doors the team must plot a sympathetic treatment that doesn't offend accepted conservation ethics but does make an item serviceable once more. Always, the starting point is consolidation, to ensure nothing further is lost. Then the experts must decide how best to honour an object's authenticity and veracity. Their duty to cultural heritage is one that's keenly felt.

For art conservator Lucia Scalisi, it's a case of combining the ethics of conservation with practicalities, for example, a ripped canvas. Above all, her aim is to impact as little as possible on an artefact, in order to preserve its integrity. No one wants their 92-year-old grandmother to have a face lift, she explains, nor do they want an eighteenth century portrait to look as if it was painted last year.

Julie Tatchell and Amanda Middleditch, the bear repairers, share those guiding principles and focus on fending off further deterioration while hoping everything they do can be undone if necessary. While they will clean a soft toy and restore missing elements, it's imperative any work they do doesn't change its personality and character. Owners want to collect the toy they have always adored, rather than a new version of it.

The Repair Shop team is united in trying to keep the patination – a top layer that forms on wood, metals and leather naturally or unavoidably over time – intact, as with it comes a sideways glance at history.

When clockwork expert Steve Fletcher set about mending a French-built steam-operated toy boat recovered years before from a sea shore, he had no qualms about ensuring the machinery inside worked safely and straightened the hull so the prop shaft would operate again. He replaced two missing masts and even added a French flag.

But although he cleaned verdigris from the 125 year old brass cannon he didn't polish them, nor did he re-paint the boat's battered bodywork so it still had the appearance of an historic object.

A moving story attached to a project tackled by carpenter Will Kirk illustrates his cautious and thoughtful approach. He was presented with a hand-carved wooden Spitfire, made by a Lancaster bomber's crewman during World War II between operations and intended for his much younger brother. When the airman was shot down and killed in 1943, on his 19th mission, the toy was finally delivered to a child and his family, now filled with heartache.

The present owner, that grieving boy's son, was himself distraught after he dropped it within days of his father's death, breaking a wing. Will immediately reassured him that both wing and tail had previously broken and he painstaking scraped away old glue before using a two-part adhesive on the repair. He cut and shaped a tiny metal fragment to replace a missing propeller shaft. But although he added paint to disguise the bonded edges of wing and tail, he left the vast majority of brushstrokes made by the ill-fated wartime airman alone, so it looked just as it would have done 75 years ago. He did however make a stand for it so it would be forever in flight and the chances of future crashes were much reduced.

Sometimes two worlds collide, however, and the experts must undertake wholesale repairs so its very survival is assured.

Brenton West is not only a silversmith but an expert in cameras and projectors. When a machine for 8mm film arrived at the workshop he put in a new bulb and drive belt. This was an occasion when restoration work went beyond a thorough clean, so a family could re-live memories captured on celluloid back in the sixties. Without his work, the projector amounted to so much metalwork. After it was completed, the machine was working as its manufacturers – and owners – intended.

One abiding guideline is that whatever is added can be taken away again, without damage. Yet metalworker Dominic Chinea's considered approach, always item-specific, might also involve safety as well as aesthetics, for example, with a toy pedal car when new pedals to replace worn ones are vital.

Whatever the challenge on the work bench, for the team of experts it's a privilege for their work to become part of an article's unfolding story and to give good order to its prolonged existence.

WOOD

E very artefact that comes into The Repair Shop has a compelling history behind it. But one object stands out for carpenter Will Kirk, for the way it dramatically changed its owner's life.

When Alan Thompson brought in a battered writing slope for renovation, there was little that highlighted its personal significance. He'd discovered it after the death of a sister, tucked under the eaves in her attic. The box was in such disrepair it almost went unnoticed.

It turned out it wasn't the box that was pivotal, but the papers Alan found inside it. Here was the official documentation that divulged that the people he knew as mum and dad were in fact his grandparents. His real mother was the woman he'd always thought of as his oldest sister.

For the first time he had evidence in his hands that laid bare a long-hidden family secret, with everyone involved apart from himself now dead. For Alan, the slope symbolised information buried and relationships unrecognised. Now Will wanted to transform the writing slope into the most beautiful, tactile treasure chest, to store those vital papers and photographs that disclosed Alan's true identity.

Although Alan had no idea about the history of his writing slope, it was certainly in a sorry state. It looked as if it had been in either a fire or a flood, with the lid charred and its veneer either missing or badly fractured.

Usually Will opts for the least abrasive cleaner, or even plain water, to remove dirt, in the hope of saving layers of polish built up over the years. In this instance it was far too late to rescue that lustre. So armed with a cotton wool bud charged with methylated spirits, he gently cleaned a corner of the box unsure of its effect. Happily, it soon revealed glossy grain and a brass inlay, which was appearing for the first time in years.

His next step was to reach for a household electric iron. After placing a cotton cloth over the lid of the box, he ironed it to both flatten down the surviving veneer and revive the original glue. That achieved better results on some parts of the lid than others, possibly because glue wasn't uniformly applied all over the lid surface in the first place. He stabilised the rest with cautiously applied wood glue, tucking it under raised veneer using a thin brush.

Then it was time to replace the missing patches of veneer. He chose cedar veneer as it acts like a blank canvas. Although it was much paler than the rest, it's far easier to make wood darker than to lighten it up.

There were two brass plates on the writing slope: one on the top and the other surrounding the lock. Both were badly tarnished, but using a cleaner with a soft cloth quickly returned them to their former glory. As well as commercially made brass cleaners, there are some tried-and-tested home-made alternatives using pantry staples that will do the job, including ketchup, yoghurt, lemon juice and bicarbonate of soda or vinegar with flour.

The leather inside the slope was beyond repair and had to be replaced with new. With tasks like these, when measurements have to be exact, Will falls back on an old Russian proverb: 'Measure seven times, cut once.' It means that extra preparation will help prevent an error and it is advice that rarely lets craftspeople down. Despite this prudent approach, he still chose PVA glue to fix it in place, as it is low-cost, strong and safe, but also gives a few moments of mobility to freely slide the surfaces into alignment before firmly clamping.

Finally, it was time to return the writing slope to Alan, the sole link he had with his newly discovered past and now a suitably significant and stylish home for mementoes of such magnitude.

TYPES OF WOOD

There are two broad categories: softwoods and hardwoods.

Not necessarily more yielding than the rest, **softwoods** are from trees that bear cones and tend to be swift growing, less dense and inexpensive.

Pine: Plantations of planted pines, with trees that reach arrow-straight for the sky, mean that it is an abundant resource. Turpentine is made from the distilled resin of some pine varieties.

Fir: An inexpensive wood that's quick to stain, fir is often used in building projects for reasons of economy.

Cedar: A reddish wood with a straight grain, cedar has a natural aroma that deters moths, making it ideal for bedroom furniture.

Versatile **hardwoods**, from broad-leaved deciduous trees, are highly prized by woodworkers for their creative potential in turning and carving. Those from warmer climates tend to emit more toxic chemicals as a defence from rampaging micro organisms.

Oak: With two recognisable hues – white and red – oak was used on Viking long ships and Britain's earliest navy vessels as it is naturally resistant to moisture and insect or fungal attack. It is characterised by its open grain.

Ash: Both resilient and bendy, this light-coloured wood has a multitude of uses, including for tool handles, baseball bats, electric guitars and even the frames of Morgan cars.

Beech: Light but rarely decorative, beech is used to make furniture carcasses, flooring and plywood. Writing in the first century AD, Roman naturalist Pliny the Elder observed, 'The wood of beech is easily worked – cut into thin layers of veneers, it is very flexible, but is only used for the construction of boxes and desks.'

Elm: A fine choice for chair seats and coffins because it's unlikely to split.

Mahogany: Its warm, reddish brown can be enhanced by either a stain or oil, but mahogany trees are now considered 'at risk' in the wild.

Rosewood: An umbrella term for a family of trees that are typified by a dark-veined, rich wood. Considered the world's most trafficked wild product, there are now international trade restrictions in place.

Teak: Naturally pest resistant, straight-grained, yellowy teak from India sometimes smells like leather and is popular among house builders as well as furniture makers as it doesn't warp.

Walnut: With its rich brown colour and tantalising grain patterns, it's often chosen for veneer.

Maple: Pale but extremely durable, this is an ideal wood to withstand wear and tear. It was another recommendation for veneer by Pliny the Elder, along with box, palm, holly and poplar.

Ebony: A favourite wood among eighteenth century French cabinet makers, its density makes it suitable for creating musical instruments as it gives good clarity.

A Selection of Will's Woodwork Tools

Few craftspeople will match the number of tools in the woodworker's workshop. Some stand like soldiers at attention in floor-to-ceiling racks, while others lie snug in a roll-up bag. Inevitably, some come to hand more than others.

1. **'Antique' screwdriver:** Old-style screws are often wider than run-of-the-mill new screwdrivers. If they are rusted into position, then only a wide, meaty screwdriver will do the job of loosening them adequately.

2. **Chisel with a maple handle:** This is ideal for jobs where the chisel is going to be struck by a hammer to shear one piece of wood away from the next, as the close-knit grain gives it strength.

3. **Chisel for wood-carving:** Choose a tool with a more ergonomically designed handle for comfort and effectiveness.

4. **Oilstone:** Craftspeople need to have the sharpest tools in the box at their disposal. With razor-edged implements the user has better control and, with the chances of slipping radically reduced, is actually less likely to cut themselves. The process of sharpening tools also helps to battle rust. Oilstones are traditionally the cheapest method and are durable.

5. **Waterstone:** Using a waterstone is usually faster for sharpening than an oilstone, with higher grades available to get sharper results.

6. **Diamond stone:** The most expensive way to sharpen your tools is to purchase a diamond stone, which, as the name implies, has industrial-strength diamonds installed in a sharpening strip.

7. **Leather strop:** Finish all blade-sharpening processes by using a leather strop to rub off minute metal filings and buff up the blade metal.

8. **Veneer hammer:** Not a hitting hammer, but a tool to smooth down veneer sheets so that excess glue is pushed to the sides.

My Favourite Tools

For some people, chisels are merely a blade on a stick. Not for Will, who bought a substantial wooden-handled, bevel edge chisel in a second-hand market in Bath recently for a tenner – but says that for him it's probably worth at least ten times that.

It has a blade made from Sheffield steel, dubbed 'rustless steel' when it was invented just prior to the First World War. While cheaper or newer chisels will quickly become blunt, this one stays sharp for the duration of a task. Lying heavy in the hand, the blade is so wide it can be used like a plane.

Of course, it's only one of many chisels in his workshop, some of which have been bought from high street chains. Cheaper tools can be used for knocking into wood that's full of nails or screws, to avoid the risk of damaging a favourite tool.

Inherited tools are the best kind, insists Will, and not just because they are free. These are tools that have already stood the test of time. Without them there are jobs that can't be done quite so well, or even at all.

PROJECTS

Like all crafts, there's a mystique surrounding woodwork that keeps even enthusiastic amateurs at bay. But Will encourages everyone to tackle projects if they feel interested and able. His advice is to spend plenty of time researching any proposed project in books and online, as there are volumes of information about woodworking available now that offer the necessary strategies.

Bear in mind that many restorers spend hours undoing work that's been badly executed, so be realistic about how much patience and application you possess.

The accessibility of the right tools and a well-lit, uncluttered workspace might also be a consideration. But the satisfaction in finishing achievable projects is immense.

If you are new to woodwork but want to get a feel for the craft, then start small. Here are some tasks that everyone can try, which will not only give the satisfaction of achievement, but could improve some of your favourite items of furniture too.

HOW TO FIX A SCRATCH ON
POLISHED WOODEN FURNITURE

1. Take an unshelled walnut and, with moderate pressure, rub it in circular motions over the scratch.

2. Rub the same area with your fingers afterwards, to warm the nut oil that's been left on the furniture's surface.

3. Wait for a few moments for the oil to seep in.

4. Buff with a soft cloth. Having been filled and coloured, the scratched area will no longer be visible.

HOW TO REMEDY A WHITE MARK
LEFT ON FURNITURE

1. A white mark means there's moisture trapped in the wood. Apply mayonnaise to the affected area and leave overnight so the vinegar-based dressing can draw the offending water out.

2. Clean with a cloth and buff. This will work for surface marks. Any indentation can only be fixed by re-polishing.

3. Invest in some coasters as they are the single best way to protect furniture from ring marks. And avoid putting plant pots at the centre of an antique table.

When chair legs buckle or table legs shear away, there's a bigger job in prospect, but not one that's necessarily out of reach. Here Will offers advice on how to effect a strong repair on broken wooden furniture.

1. Make sure the facing sides of the item being glued are clean and dust free.

2. Apply the glue so there's enough to cover the surface and sufficient even to soak into the wood. However, ensure it doesn't form a gluey wedge, as this will stop the wood holding together after it has adhered and will become a weakness.

3. Remember that glue has an 'open' time, when it is liquid and workable, so be prepared to work in a timely manner before it turns to gel.

4. Clamp the repair as effectively as possible. That means applying firm pressure on the repaired area so that the glue can dry with everything locked into the proper place.

5. Leave for 12 hours or in line with the glue manufacturer's recommendations.

HOW TO REPAIR RAISED VENEER

In an arid land where trees were a rarity, the Ancient Egyptians began using veneer to make the most of a scarce resource. Those limited amounts of timber available to them were cut into wafer-thin sheets and fixed to other, less precious surfaces to give the illusion of solid wood. The same principles have been applied for centuries afterwards, with inexpensive furniture carcasses expertly hidden behind a glossy and luxuriant veneer exterior. To get a satisfactory result using veneer over a large area almost certainly means employing a hydraulic press or a vacuum bag to apply the necessary pressure while the glue is drying. However, as veneer quickly dries out, with rosewood being amongst the driest, it can raise over time and look unsightly. And this is a repair that can be carried out without specialist tools.

1. To achieve the best finish, clear away any traces of old glue on both surfaces.

2. Glue made from the collagen of animals, found in bones and hide, is the best for the job. Professional restorers use hot animal glue, which must be mixed with care, responds to temperature and comes in different strengths. Instead, choose a liquid hide glue, which comes ready-made and can be applied with relative ease by a paintbrush.

3. Press down the stray veneer and wipe away any excess glue.

4. Clamp the repaired area while the glue is setting. Use masking tape to hold the veneer in place in areas that are too tricky to clamp.

HOW TO FRENCH POLISH

French polishing is the process by which a distinctive gloss is applied to wooden furniture, using numerous coats of shellac mixed with methylated spirits. Despite years of experience in French polishing, Will still considers his biggest workshop challenge is to accurately reproduce the patination – the shine and the antique depth – that distinguishes this furniture. It's something that may take a hundred years to form, and it is gone in an instant if an uninformed restorer makes the wrong choices.

French polishing isn't necessarily the preserve of professionals, but given that getting the right colour and shine by mixing wax and polish to the existing pigments in the wood is a real test even for the experts, this is an art that needs to be well practiced. If you have a piece of unloved furniture and want to give French polishing a try, you can mirror Will's steps.

1. Before applying the polish there's preparation to be done, which involves stripping off the old varnish or wax and rubbing down with fine abrasive paper. It's a time-consuming job, but a necessary one to offer a blank, smooth, blemish-free canvas for the polish.

2. To fill in any open grain, Will rubs chalk dust into the surface (although grainy marks will fade more with every coat of polish).

3. Mix commercially made shellac polish with methylated spirits – using about a kilo of polish to five litres of spirit – before applying it with something called a French polishing rubber or fad. In fact it's not a rubber, so much as a material bung.

Make your own by taking a square of lint-free scrap cotton and choosing some cheesecloth or fine-grade waste cotton for the centre. Soak the cheesecloth cotton in polish before pulling up the corners of its material hammock and twisting, ensuring there are no creases on the bottom, to make a pear-shaped pad. Now it should move freely on the surface, with the polish oozing gently through the outer cotton cover to leave a thin and even coat along the grain of the wood in its wake. It's important to squeeze any excess polish out before starting.

4. Work from one side of an object to the next to avoid making an initial landing mark, which will be difficult to remove. In further applications, when a coating has been established, use multiple figure-of-eight motions. When the surface feels sticky and drags on the rubber, it's time to leave the article to dry. It takes at least a week for it to dry before work can begin again.

5. To achieve the smoothness and shine associated with French polishing, the final layers are built up with shellac thinned further still with methylated spirits. This needs to be applied in quick motion across the surface, in a process known as flashing off. In effect, this melts the polish to create a reflective shine.

HALLMARKS OF THE ERA

Through the ages wooden furniture has reflected much more than merely domestic style. It's a fusion of international history and technological advance that mirrors society's evolution. While it's not possible to investigate it thoroughly here, there are clues incorporated in this flying visit around furniture history that might help you date an old family favourite.

16TH AND 17TH CENTURIES

Rudimentary furniture existed in Britain before Tudor times but it was then that chunky, carved pieces came to prominence. Dubbed the age of oak, it began in about 1500 and lasted a century, although surviving pieces like four-poster beds and throne-style chairs were originally the preserve of nobility.

It encompassed the Jacobean period, defined by backed armchairs, hall cupboards, settles and framed chests. The most opulent of these had mother of pearl inlays, which all became more abundant.

The era gave way to the age of walnut, reflecting an advance in sawing techniques that permitted thinner planking, yielding a better return on wood. In turn the science of fitted drawers took a leap forward.

By the middle of the eighteenth century the most fashionable new furniture was made of mahogany and satinwood. Following European expansion into the New World, the rich depth of newly discovered mahogany and honey tones of satinwood were soon in high demand. Early in the century, the taste had been elegantly simple furniture thanks to the high cost of the wood and overarching Puritan ethics. But transport innovation increased the opportunities for import and in 1788 alone 30,000 tons of satinwood was brought into England and Wales from the West Indies.

Before his death in 1779, Yorkshire-born Thomas Chippendale had set a benchmark for carpenters everywhere, reflecting Gothic, Chinese and French rococo styles popular at the time in his widely distributed pattern book The Gentleman and Cabinet Maker's Director.

The increase in ornamentation is bracketed as the Baroque period, a response by the Catholic church to the Protestant Reformation which included the use of extravagant inlays and extensive gilding. It came to Britain with an influx of craftspeople when travelling around Europe became more commonplace.

By 1800, decoration was richer and more imaginative even for workaday furniture including, for example, cabriole legs curved outwards at the shoulder and inwards at the feet. A plain pad was replaced by hooves, ball and claw and then scroll designs.

In the Regency period, prior to Queen Victoria taking the throne, the popularity of rosewood grew. And as education began to shine a light on greater numbers of the population, the demand for desks and especially writing slopes rose. Also called lap desks, they were personal possessions rather than furniture that were taken on military campaigns or overseas tours and used to write novels, letters, contracts and postcards.

They could store the fundamentals of old-style communication. Some have glass inkwells or secret drawers and may have once housed gentlemen's shaving or women's sewing kits alongside pens and paper. These small, shiny chests are frequently decorated with brass, mother of pearl or marquetry.

Bamboo furniture appeared for the first time in the 1740s but enjoyed peak popularity in Victorian times. The same applies to caned chairs.

It was during the latter half of the nineteenth century that furniture styles turned and turned again. For the first time painted furniture began to appeal to home-owners, either to disguise an inexpensive wood or mimic a rare one.

Plywood, formed from gluing thin sheets of wood together, came to the fore in the 1860s not as board but moulded, in furniture. Not only was it cheaper than forest-hewn wood but it could be used in mass produced items.

In the distant past, castors had been made of wood and then leather but finally brass castors made bulky furniture easy to manoeuvre. Now mass production associated with the Industrial Revolution made items much cheaper and easier to obtain. With manufacturers striving to gain prominence in a competitive market, there was a perpetual cycle of revivals of previous fashions, making it difficult for a lay person to distinguish an original Queen Anne piece from a Victorian imitation.

20TH CENTURY

The Arts and Crafts movement, in full flight by the turn of the twentieth century, was a response to this, emphasising the need for integrity, beauty and craftsmanship.

During the twentieth century there were a range of furniture designs queuing to take a bow centre stage, including Edwardian style, more compact than previously to fit into the rafts of new homes built for the burgeoning middle classes, and Art Deco, with its simplified forms. Mid-century it was modernism that was popular: striking yet functional. In Britain downbeat utility furniture was the order of the day as far as the government was concerned, to help manage a wartime shortage in timber. And it was these inexpensive pieces that became familiar to many as they grew up, earning a place in their hearts that no showstopper piece could rival.

Memorable Moments

....

Will: 'Every piece has its own story. It is amazing to think that some of my work becomes part of that story.'

The oldest piece of furniture to have come through The Repair Shop doors is a Georgian knee-hole desk that had been in the same family from new and was handed down through the female line.

It fell to Will Kirk to return this 'cherished old lady' to tip-top condition before it went on to the next generation. He identified it as an early Georgian piece of furniture, approximately dating from the reign of George I, between 1714 and 1727. Soon afterwards, furniture fashion came under the broad influence of interior designer Thomas Chippendale, and walnut gave way to mahogany while ball and claw feet replaced traditional squared ones.

Although its top featured ink stains, coffee cup rings and veneer chips and there was evidence of a previous wood worm infestation, the desk still stood firmly on its own four feet. So it was rejuvenating care that was required rather than anything structural.

Perhaps the most challenging task for Will was to replace a top corner of the desk devoured long ago by wood-worm. The tell-tale pattern of tiny holes in a patch of wood left spongy by the attack meant it would be impossible to satisfactorily mask the area with a 'sticking plaster' approach. The corner would have to be removed and replaced. After cutting away the damaged section Will found a piece of solid walnut that he could glue into place. Much later, when the glue was dry, he used chisels to carve it into an exact match for the opposite corner.

Missing veneer doesn't usually present a difficulty. This time, though, the historic veneer was cut much thicker than its modern equivalents and Will initially struggled to find a match with sufficient depth to create a smooth finish. When that hurdle was overcome, the carefully selected veneer was held in place by masking tape while the glue dried. Only then could he file it to fit, then colour match it.

Like all furniture, the desk had attracted its fair share of dirt down the centuries. Repeated polishing can trap the gathered grime under a sheen but Will was determined to refresh its appearance, so its colours would be richer and deeper. Using a rag armed with a mild mix of white spirit and turpentine the muck of ages was slowly stripped away before its final polish. In doing so he retained ingrained marks that added to its character while giving it a lustre worthy of its historic status.

* * *

Still, there's no set pattern to the way Will works. When another wooden heirloom came his way he began, rather than ended, his work with a deep clean. This three-legged table had a triangular top which was transformed into a circle when three curved, hinged flaps were lifted into position. The flaps, all in excellent condition, were decorated with inlay. But the top had a central section of veneer missing, probably lifted by the dampness of a plant pot placed there at some stage in its 200-year history.

Immediately Will identified it as a rosewood table, which presented a difficulty. It's a wood that becomes lighter with age and the dark replacement veneer would not sit well among the more aged blond wood surrounding it. Reluctantly, Will decided on a two-stage process bleaching for the strips of veneer he had chosen, something he only uses as a last resort as it's such a caustic and powerful substance. However, once the treated wood was neutralised with a mix of water and white spirit the effect was everything he'd hoped for: smooth, pale and beautifully patterned. Still, he had yet to tackle the challenge of making a seamless repair at the table's heart.

On closer inspection he discovered that the veneer surround the missing patch was mottled and grey – and he called in ceramics expert Kirsten Ramsey for a second opinion. Should he continue with the difficult-to-manage repair or take a bolder route, replacing all the veneer on the table top that was encased in a thread of decorative inlay? After scrutinising the existing veneer, Kirsten appreciated why he was having second thoughts about a small-scale repair. Scalpel in hand, Will began the slow task of removing it all.

Happily, he knew one effective short cut to lift the thin wood from strong, stable adhesive that had endured for decades. With a damp cloth on the table he brandished a warm iron to ease off each section, careful not to impinge on the inlay.

Soon the exposed base wood was re-covered with the treated strips of veneer, cut after being measured – and re-measured – to ensure it was correctly placed. After each side of the triangle was glued, a plank of wood was clamped across it to ensure it dried flat.

The result was impressive, but Will was quickly distracted by a different issue. One of the side flaps stood proud of the table, creating a ridge. When he investigated he realised the some of the hinges were bent with age so these too were clamped to make them straight again.

With a final polish the table was revived to its pre-Victorian splendour, in a condition that the owner's great grandmother would recognise and one that his descendants would appreciate.

* * *

Sometimes it's experience that brings about the right results, at other times, plain instinct. But as with the table, occasionally Will has to rely on the expertise of others to guide him.

That's what happened when he was presented with a broken spinning wheel, once used for tourist displays on the Shetland Islands. When he surveyed the treadle-powered device he admitted he was 'on the ropes' as he had no idea what a working model looked like.

As part of his research he consulted with Joan and Clive Jones, who have been restoring spinning wheels for more than 20 years. Joan explained the spinning wheels from Shetland comprised various woods. As there were no trees on Shetland, makers were historically dependent on what washed up on the shores.

She explained the broken 'flyer', a U-shaped part with a metal shaft which holds the bobbin and helps wind the yarn, would need to be refashioned rather than repaired as the centrifugal force it created would defy any adhesive.

Copying the intact side of the flyer on to graph paper and flipping it to draw its second, broken arm, Will then cut out a replacement and shaped it on a lathe. With the wobbly base below, he pulled out each leg with ease, the connecting adhesive having crumbled. After cleaning out the dried glue he stuck it together again, ensuring the base was horizontal and stable this time. Always appreciative of team work, Will welcomed Joan and Clive back to The Repair Shop to ensure the spinning wheel was working well before it was returned to its owners.

USEFUL TERMS

Flitch: A log that has been made into veneer sheets, which are bundled together and ready to use in the order they were cut. It's a good idea to number these sheets, to ensure they stay in their running order.

Clipped: Sheets of veneer where the defects have been removed.

Intarsia: Italian Renaissance technique by which sawn veneers were laid into solid wood. Today, it equates to marquetry.

Cross banding: A wide strip of straight-grained veneer, used as a frame for veneer panels, sometimes edged with decorative bandings.

Feather matching: Using straight-grained veneer in a chevron shape.

Ormolu: Also known as firegilding, ormolu refers to the metallic mounts that were hallmarks of French cabinet makers in the eighteenth and nineteenth century. Originally, ormolu was a gold and mercury amalgam applied to bronze. However, the mercury component meant gilders rarely survived into their middle years, so the original materials were sidelined in favour of less-harmful copper and zinc.

Rotary cut veneer: Once veneer was hand-sawn, but technology meant that veneer factories appeared from the middle of the nineteenth century. Soon mahogany nut and rosewood veneers, with their rich colours and complex grains, became affordable and desirable. Today the thickness of veneer can be as thin as a flimsy 0.5mm by rotary cutting the tree trunk using a modern machine as if it were a pencil being sharpened.

Shellac: Collected from the bark of trees in India and Thailand after being secreted by a bug, shellac comes in dried flakes and is mixed into polish.

Will's List of Do's and Don'ts

- *Don't put wooden furniture in windows, where it's in the path of direct sunlight, or next to radiators. The heat will shrink wood and warp veneer. Even in an old piece of furniture, the wood is still living. The contraction of wooden furniture is also a hazard with underfloor heating.*

- *Do dust wooden furniture often, but don't use aerosol furniture polish that contains silicone as this may burn through the top layer of polish and create a hazing effect.*

- *Do apply a beeswax polish with a soft cloth every six months.*

- *Do pick up chairs from under the seat, rather than the back, so there's no undue pressure put on the joints.*

- *Don't lift a table from the top surface in case that loosens its fixings to the base. Choose the legs instead.*

- *Don't pull a drawer open with one handle as this will open it at an angle and can harm the runners and joints.*

SILVERWARE

A dmired for centuries, lustrous silver is still highly sought after for making jewellery and other decorative objects. A collection belonging to one household was deemed so desirable a burglar put almost all of it into his swag bag, leaving a family devastated. The sole remaining item of the inherited silver was a mirror with a blue velvet border smothered in shiny decor, with one top corner on its ornate border damaged – which is perhaps why the thief left it behind.

No one knows the age of the silverware or how the mirror frame was broken but, with the rest of the collection gone, its sentimental value was vastly enhanced. Carol New bought it into The Repair Shop to see if the small but significant section of missing silver could be recreated.

For silversmith Brenton West it was a challenging prospect, but one for which he had special empathy. In 1980, items he fashioned during a three year silversmithing course in Kent were stolen while they were on display in the foyer of a top London hotel, so he recognised the sense of loss this family felt.

Still, it wasn't a case of merely mimicking another corner as the intricate pattern surrounding the mirror rendered a different formation on each one. He had noticed it was at least a repeating pattern, so with careful observation he could deduce what was missing. Now he combined the ancient craft of silversmithing with some new technology to achieve the results he needed. After photographing the section of pattern he wanted to recreate, he used computer software to put it into the shape of a corner. For the first time he saw the proper formation of the missing link.

After tracing the computer-made pattern he could lay it directly on to a piece of silver. Decorations like this are made by a process called chasing, using punches with shaped ends. Chasing tools come in various sizes and designs and if Brenton doesn't have the one he needs to hand, he will make one that's right for the job. By tapping on the punch Brenton could mould the metal and create raised reliefs. The sliver of silver needs to be held firm while that's being done, however, so Brenton reached for some specialist kit, a cast-iron pot filled with malleable pitch. Heated until it's molten, the pitch holds the silver like glue while work is being done, but doesn't hinder the pattern-making process.

Approaching from the top, he sank small sections of the metal, leaving a protruding pattern. When a similar procedure is carried out on the reverse side of the silver, it is known as repousse. It's time-consuming but, with limited changes since the third century BC when the first evidence of the craft appeared, it's a living link with all the great civilisations of the past in which decorative metalwork was prized, including the Egyptians and the Incas.

To liberate the elaborate outline he'd forged from its original silver rectangle, he chose a jeweller's piercing saw with a blade little wider than a single hair. Exerting only mild pressure, he cut downwards to create the spaces that would reveal glimpses of the blue velvet behind the silver border. Inevitably tiny slithers of silver were lost to the floor. Brenton collects these for a scrap pot, the contents of which are recycled annually.

The sight of the fixed and freshly polished looking glass stirred powerful emotions, this time not for the loss the family had suffered, but sheer joy that this splendid memento would be saved for future generations.

Hallmarks

A set of symbols on precious metals that guarantee its purity. They include marks that denote the Assay Office where the article was tested, the name of the maker and the date it was made. Additional marks might also reveal if it was a commemorative item, whether it was imported and if duty has been paid. The system of publishing the provenance of the silver to safeguard the metal's value has been in existence for more than 700 years.

A Selection of Brenton's Workshop Tools

Silver is soft and pliable, which dictates some of the more unusual articles in his collection.

1. **Leather sandbag:** A firm cushion against which Brenton can mould silver.

2. **Pitch bowl:** To hold silver while work is carried out.

3. **Ring mandrel:** A round form used for making rings.

4. **Files:** To smooth imperfections from the metal before polishing.

5. **Punches:** An array, all of which he has made.

6. **Soldering equipment:** Silver is notoriously difficult to solder, but some repairs dictate it must be done. For example, old silver spoons that may fracture can have the split sawn out, hammered down and soldered to effect an invisible repair.

7. **Piercing saw:** Rather than large wood saws, Brenton's tend to have delicate frames and minute blades.

My Favourite Tools

Not just one but three tools are rated as essentials by Brenton when he's in his workshop. First of the trio is a doming hammer, which he would use to make a pot or vase out of a flat silver sheet in a bowl-shaped indent formed in the cross-section of a tree trunk.

Next is the raising hammer, used to 'raise' the metal by hammering on cast-iron stakes.

Finally, there's the planishing hammer, used to smooth a surface by lightly tapping so that each hammer mark overlaps the last.

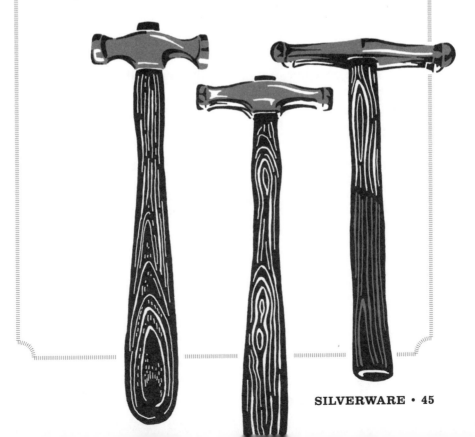

PROJECTS

HOW TO POLISH SILVER

1. Don't use the wrong polish on silver as those made for brass or other metals are too abrasive. Specially designated silver polish is less so.

2. Use a soft cloth and a small amount of polish.

3. Rub the cloth in an up-and-down motion, rather than a circular one, which risks abrasion.

4. Turn the cloth frequently so there's no chance of putting back the tarnish taken from one item on to another.

5. Be careful polishing around the silver hallmark. A sustained campaign of vigorous polishing could render the mark illegible.

6. Rinse and buff.

7. There are numerous suggestions for cleaning silver using household goods. However, the advantage with polish is that it guards against tarnish and slows its encroachment.

HOW TO REPAIR A SCRATCH
IN A SILVER ITEM*

1. Only use this technique on everyday silver items. Seek professional help regarding valuable pieces.

2. Soak some very fine wet and dry sandpaper (2,000 grade) and work it gently over the scratch.

3. When the scratch has disappeared from view, use even finer wet and dry sandpaper (4,000) and repeat the process to rid the item of any residual marks.

4. Next, take some brass or chrome cleaner and use vigorously on the area.

5. Finally, use dedicated silver polish to refine the finish.

* Do not use on silver-plated items

HOW TO REFURBISH BRASS DOOR KNOBS

Brass door furnishings are found in houses old and new. In Victorian times, unlacquered brass was relentlessly polished to keep it shiny, although today a degree of natural tarnish is sometimes seen as lending character. Modern equivalents are usually lacquered, eliminating the need for regular maintenance.

1. Lacquered brass has a clear protective sheen. Dust with a soft cloth and do not use polish.

2. If black spots have started appearing on a lacquered item it indicates the lacquer is breaking down. The same is true if dull patches are evolving.

3. To remove failing lacquer, Brenton uses acetone or alcohol and works in a well-ventilated room, wearing goggles. In addition to commercially-made solutions, bicarbonate of soda and boiling water will also strip it back. Use a stiff brush – not one with metal bristles that could leave scratch marks – to remove stubborn stains.

4. You can then choose to leave the door knobs unlacquered and commit to a regular polishing regime. This will be especially necessary if the brassware is exposed to weather and body oils from skin.

5. Or you might prefer to re-lacquer, either immediately or later after ensuring the surface is clean so a new layer will properly adhere.

6. There's a chance your door handle isn't solid brass. Test with a magnet. If it sticks to the handle then it's a ferrous metal underneath with a brass finish, which could be rubbed away by over-polishing. If the magnet doesn't stick, double check by making a small scratch in a hidden area. Should the scratch mark show up a silvery colour, then it indicates the item is also brass-plated. In both instances, a lacquered finish is probably the better option.

MEMORABLE MOMENTS

Brenton: 'In these days of efficient manufacturing processes our thoughts have been drawn away from the skill of the craftsman. My job is to entice people back into appreciating the dexterity of the hands and the efforts of minds that created items that I repair.'

In Wales a love of poetry, prose and music is celebrated in Eisteddfod festivals across the country in a tradition that dates back to the Middle Ages.

One 15-year-old was proud to win the silver crown adorned with a red velvet cap for her poetry recitation in 1937. Eventually she passed both the silver-plated diadem and a love of performance art to her daughter. But the engraved crown came off second best as it got dented and bent when it was stored in a box. The task of reviving the tarnished prize fell to silversmith Brenton West who started by giving it a thorough clean. His next move was to pass the velvet insert, now parted from the crown, to the bear repair duo Julie and Amanda for cleaning and renovation.

The crown was a compressed oval instead of being head-shaped. Rather than squeeze the crown this way and that, Brenton cut a strip of brass and formed it into a pattern that would fit his head, to use as a guide. As he discovered, the crown with its nickel base was tough to manipulate. He pressed it against his leather sandbag, constantly checking it against the brass ring until the shape was properly refined.

Then he cleaned the crown again, this time using a finely textured Water of Ayr Stone. Also known as a Tam O'Shanter hone, Scotch or snakestone, it was first quarried north of the border, and then mined. Always used in conjunction with water to stop it scratching, the hone stone is used for both polishing and sharpening. Afterwards he could clearly see where the silver plate had worn away and the nickel beneath was showing through.

To rectify that Brenton used silver plating solution, with an electric charge running through the crown to make it adhere.

As for the red velvet cap, it was now itself in two parts. Amanda washed the lush material in mild suds while Julie reinforced the separated band with a strip of felt, that was then covered by the original satin. The two parts were then sewn together and returned to Brenton so he could glue it into the crown, where it once again stood proud of the rim.

The crown was now gleaming and plush, a regal addition to Welsh cultural history.

* * *

The small silver purse, used to hold mementos of a mum long gone and barely known, had seen better days. It was discoloured by time, and pock-marked by dings, with a leather inset that was frail and flapping.

Crumpled and dulled, it sat in the palm of Brenton's hand while he considered how to tackle a project that held special significance for a woman who was 22 when her mother died, as the deep-rooted maternal bond was poised to bloom into a loving, giving friendship.

None of his plans could materialise, though, until Susie stepped in to remove the leather purse sections which were so finely folded they looked like origami. She gently levered the leatherwork off its thin cardboard backing to give herself a pattern to follow while making a replacement.

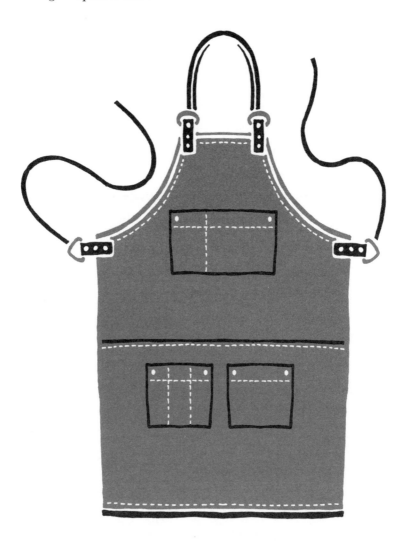

Back in Brenton's hands the lightweight purse had its small chain handle removed as well as the pin hinge. With each separated side he now embarked on the process of annealing, heating and cooling the silver to make it more malleable. In turn he warmed the tree resin in his pitch pot, which acted like a supportive hand beneath each curved side as he tapped out the lumps and bumps of the thin and brittle silver. It was a painstaking process. Working on the inside of the purse, he used a hammer and a chasing tool, striking it gently to achieve minute movements in the metal. Inevitably, that caused tiny ripples on its outside, visible despite the lined pattern. To counter those Brenton turned the purse sides over and used smaller taps still, working between the lines for a smooth finish. Then it came to polishing which finally revealed the evenness in the shaped halves that he had been working towards.

He poked the hinge pin back into place using parallel pliers before returning it to Susie so she could reunite it with the leather insert. She had recreated the three internal compartments after grasping the way it was folded and stitched, and now carefully glued it back into place. When the chain was attached it looked just as it did when its first owner saw it. Soon the family treasures were nestling inside once more: a Victorian crown said to be an unknown grandfather's first week's wages and a mother's wedding ring.

USEFUL TERMS

EPNS: Stands for Electro Plated Nickel Silver and refers to the base metal of an item, which might have been silver plated. The name is misleading as there's no silver involved, rather an alloy of nickel, zinc and copper.

Annealing: Heating and quenching metal to make it more malleable.

Bezel: A grooved ring that holds the cover of a watch face, photograph or a locket in place.

Lemel: Scraps of silver.

Chasing: A metalwork technique in which soft metal is gently hammered to create patterns.

Repousse or repoussage: A metalwork technique in which the metal is gently hammered from its underside into a pattern.

Brenton's List of Do's and Don'ts

- *Don't put valuable or old silver in the dishwasher. This is particularly true of antique dinner service knives, which have handles filled with pitch resin that melts at high temperatures. In modern silver knives that's been replaced by epoxy resin.*

- *Do put cleaned silver that's not destined for a shelf in an airtight container to help maintain its lustre.*

- *Don't attempt to fix silver with lead solder. Lead quickly corrodes silver.*

- *Don't eat eggs with silver cutlery as the sulphur in them turns silverware black.*

LEATHER

In 1967 a suspended chair went on sale that seemed to characterise both easy living and the ethos of the decade. Instantly it became a design icon. Called the Leaf Chair, for the shape of the seat that dangled in a white, powder-coated steel frame, its designer was Rupert Oliver, the pioneer of soft play equipment.

So perhaps it was fitting that the chair, which became a fixture of Carl Sebastian's childhood, was not so much high fashion furniture as a rocking boat that he sailed with his sisters and cousins when he visited his Italian grandmother's flat, where the chair was hung in reach of the record player. Eventually Carl was given it when his *nonna* downsized.

But, as the years passed, the chair became less of a boat and more like a leaky tub. The leather turned increasingly brittle until it was finally reduced to chunky shreds, flapping from leather lacing that held them fast to the frame.

The Repair Shop's leather expert, Suzie Fletcher, was left scratching her head about the best way to make this exemplar piece of furniture shipshape again without sacrificing one iota of its comfort. Usually, craftspeople prefer to maintain the original materials in a restoration project, but this time the buffalo hide was beyond repair so an all-new seat had to be fashioned. However, the original design was far from straightforward, using three seamed sections to create a clever bowl shape that cradled the body. Now the challenge was to ensure a seat replacement didn't ride too high on the frame, nor was slung too low. Fortunately, upholstery guru Sonaaz Nooronvary was on hand with feedback and ideas.

The way forward, Sonaaz felt, was to make a pattern from calico and tape it to the frame so they could use nips and tucks to test width and depth, and see just how the three-section seat would look before making any inroads into a costly leather hide. It was time well-spent as the pattern seemed to be a perfect replica. Immediately, the margin for error was substantially reduced and Suzie could cut out the shapes with certainty – although not before she triple-checked measurements for this monumental project.

Suzie realised she would have to use a piece of full grain leather, the tough top layer of a hide, to ensure the seat stood up to wear and tear. Folding, sewing and trimming the seams on each of the three sections was a relatively straightforward task for a seasoned stitcher like Suzie, but when she joined them together, the animal skins became bulky and difficult to manoeuvre, especially as they were being machine-sewn. The seams would be the backbone of the new seat, taking all the strain, so even and strong stitching was essential. With Sonaaz at her side, she wrestled the leather through the sewing machine at a snail's pace.

As a master saddler, Suzie is used to heavy work, which was fortunate as the onerous job of punching 100 holes around the edges of the new seat and securing brass eyelets in them still lay ahead. It was a time-consuming process. Only then could she finish the job, threading yards of leather thonging between seat and frame to hold it secure.

Carl and his Italian *nonna* were delighted with the chair, while for Suzie there was a different satisfaction. She had not only tested her craftsmanship, but also learned something new, having collaborated with Sonaaz. For her, it's not the amount of certificates she keeps in a drawer that pay tribute to her ability and professionalism, but the excellence of the last job she did.

TANNING

Tanning is the process that turns animal hides into leather. Without it the skin would putrefy, and historically tanners were relegated to the outskirts of villages and towns because of the noxious smells associated with their craft. Although it's a far less malodorous job today, the necessary steps to turn skin to supple material are much the same.

1. The first step is to cure the hide, by salting or chilling, which not only arrests further deterioration but also removes water content. This can take anything from hours to days.

2. The hide is then soaked in water to rehydrate and clean it.

3. Liming then takes place, to remove the outer layer of skin and hair. It also helps to eliminate grease and fat while conditioning the skin. Any remaining hair is taken off either by machine or by hand using a knife, in a process known as scudding.

4. Afterwards the hide goes through a machine to remove any remaining fleshy tissue.

5. Now the alkalines are neutralised to stabilise the skin's tissues, in what's known as deliming.

6. That's followed by bating, a softening process once carried out with animal dung, but now with the use of enzymes.

7. Then it's time to pickle the hide, first using a salt solution, then a weak acid, to bring down its pH.

8. Degreasing using solvents takes out the last of the excess fat prior to tanning.

9. There are several different processes when it comes to tanning. Mostly chromium salts are used to make stretchy leather suitable for clothes or handbags. However, tanning with different chemicals or even plant extracts also takes place. In all cases the hides are neutralised afterwards to remove any remaining chemicals.

10. At this point the leather might be dyed.

11. Afterwards comes fatliquoring, that is, applying oils to lubricate the fibres and keep the leather supple.

12. Samming is the process of putting the hide through a large mangle-style machine to remove water.

13. Setting out means the leather is stretched and smoothed. Together with the next process of final drying, the water content is further reduced.

14. A staking machine massages the leather to make it softer. It might even be subjected to dry drumming, being tumbled in a rotating drum, for the same purpose. Now the surface is reading for mechanical abrasion if it is destined to be suede, or buffing, to produce a fine nap. All leather is graded before it is despatched.

A SELECTION OF SUZIE'S HAND TOOLS

1. **Knives:** Suzie uses round, head, straight and French knives.

2. **Plough gauge:** This cuts strips of leather to a specific width.

3. **Awls:** These come in various sizes and are used for making holes.

4. **Pricking iron:** In hand-sewing, this is used to mark stitch length and size.

5. **Crew punches:** These come in various sizes, to make rectangular holes for buckle tongues.

6. **Edge tool:** This removes the sharp edges of recently cut leather.

7. **Edge creaser:** A heated iron used to put a line on leather, either for decoration or as a guide for stitching.

8. **Splitting machine:** Also known as a skiving machine, it slices thick leather to create two layers.

9. **Flocking iron:** Once used to position specially tufted wool in saddle panels and seats. Today, wool has been largely replaced by foam.

10. **Smasher:** This is used to flatten the wool going into the saddle.

The tool kit also includes assorted hammers, mallets, rulers, needles, punches and a staple gun.

My Favourite Tools

As a teenager, Suzie had a workshop in her grandparents' house, in a room that had once belonged to her father. One of the first tools she used there was a pair of pliers with red plastic handles and a narrow head. At the time they belonged her grandfather – the clock repairer who inspired her brother Steve – but they soon became part of her tool kit and are still in regular use today. Although part of the plastic handle has come away, the tool's head remains shiny and its ridged teeth are intact. For Suzie, having them is like maintaining a tangible connection with him.

She also feels that craftspeople are so at one with their tools that they can identify each by feel. Every awl, knife and pricking iron has its place on her workshop walls. She has even been known to cry when an often-used and much-loved one breaks.

1. 'The Beast' is the name of Suzie's heavy-duty sewing machine, a German-made Adler, which can stitch through tough and thick leather 'as if it were butter'.

2. By contrast, 'Edith' is a medium-weight machine for less robust projects, once again made in Germany.

3. Her third machine is called 'Pearl', a 29K Singer treadle machine, made for industrial use and with a revolving foot so it can sew in any direction. Her serial number reveals that 'Pearl' was one of 2,000 machines of this type that were made in 1951. Suzie admits it is sometimes difficult to work with the historic machine, but respects Pearl because of her great age.

4. Suzie has a cobblers' 'last' called 'James', with three arms that are shaped like human feet, used for shoemaking.

5. Emptying her father's workshop after his death, Suzie picked up more small pliers and nippers, which she didn't know she would need, but would be lost without today.

Since being part of The Repair Shop team, Suzie has learned hot foil embossing in order to decorate a rocking horse's reins. She taught herself the skill after the rocking horse was bought in for renovation by a woman whose husband, like Suzie's, had died from cancer. Now she has a number of embossing wheels in her tool collection, which she uses to imprint gold or coloured foils on to leather.

PROJECTS

Few craftspeople will have as many tools in their locker as leather workers like Suzie. Since learning her skills at a seven year apprenticeship after school, she has gathered an array of tools to cover every eventuality. Still, there are maintenance routines and small repair jobs that are within everyone's grasp thanks to Suzie's guidance.

HOW TO CLEAN AND 'FEED' LEATHER

When leather loses all its natural oils, there's a risk it will crack. When leather becomes riven with cracks that are deep and well-established, it could break. Using a conditioner will help replenish it with appropriate grease, to make it supple again and add resilience. A good leather conditioner will also provide a stain repellent barrier, brings out the natural shine rather than changing the colour of the leather and won't feel sticky. Depending on the item, it might be best to look for a conditioner that offers UV protection.

1. Dip a clean, soft cloth in tepid water and squeeze to remove excess moisture.

2. Wipe it over the leather in broad sweeps, gradually turning the cloth so it picks up all the surface dust, mud, sweat and grease. If you are cleaning shoes, be sure all the dirt is gone from seams and beneath laces because the sand and grit embedded in there act like sandpaper.

3. If there's a stain, wipe over a larger area instead of concentrating on one spot, to avoid soaking the patch with water or marking the surface by rubbing too vigorously.

4. Don't use harsh cleaners or abrasive tools, even if that seems right for the job. There's a risk the leather will be scratched, discoloured or frayed.

5. When it's clean, let the item air-dry. Don't be tempted to put it by a radiator or in the sun to quicken the process as that may compromise the leather.

6. For saddlery, solid cases and harnesses, Suzie recommends bar saddle soap. Once again, wring out a clean cloth, rub it on the bar and then apply to the leather. It both feeds and protects the leather, leaving it supple and glossy.

7. Now it's time to finish the job with a coat of conditioner. If the item comes into contact with clothing – like belts, furniture seats, car interiors or handbags – make sure the formula you use won't come off on your clothes. Suitable products usually come as a cream that's wiped on, left to dry and wiped over again afterwards. Test creams on a small and unseen patch before use. Don't overdo it when you apply conditioner though. If the fibres of the leather become saturated they become prone to overstretching and disfigurement. Overstretched leather cannot be restored to full health.

8. Let a thin layer of purpose-made conditioner sit on shoes until it is absorbed. Afterwards, use shoe polish, which will help seal in the newly added oil, then buff to a shine.

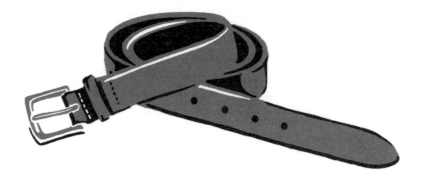

HOW TO MAKE AN EXTRA HOLE IN YOUR BELT

Losing weight, or gaining it, could render a well-loved belt unusable. Add an extra hole to give it a new lease of life by following these simple steps.

1. To avoid injury, use the right tool for the job. You need a rotary hole punch, available from tack shops, shoe shops or online for as little as £10. Its wheel will have six different sizes of hole punch.

2. Mark the belt where you need a new hole and choose the appropriate size hole punch to create it.

3. Line up the hole punch and squeeze its pliers-style handles. Some effort will be needed, depending on the thickness of the belt. It might be helpful to pull the leather around the punch to be sure it cuts cleanly through.

HOW TO MEND A HANDBAG

With bags and briefcases, a timely stitch will either effect a temporary repair – to stop it getting worse before you get a professional's help – or mend it so it is ready for use again.

1. Assemble everything you need. The problem has started with worn thread, so the first thing to locate is a heavy-duty one, which you will find on sale in tack shops or at shoe repairers. In addition, you will need a blunt end needle – which is typically stubby with a large eye – a piece of beeswax and a pair of scissors.

2. Pull out all the loose thread and, if it's possible, knot it with the thread ends still attached to the bag to stop it unravelling further.

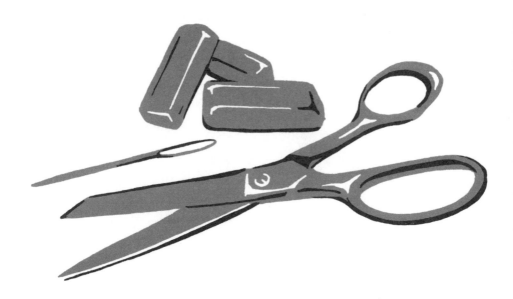

3. Cut a piece of thread long enough to go two and a half times the gap that needs sewing.

4. Run the thread through a piece of beeswax so it's better protected as it is pulled through the leather.

5. Using holes that already exist, thread up the needle and start by pulling the thread through the first hole for half of its length.

6. Start sewing using each hole, with this half of the thread, in a running stitch, pulling the thread tight.

7. At the end of the line of stitches, unthread the needle and return to the unused half-length of thread. Now use this to stitch in reverse. When it's complete there should running stitches between holes on both sides of the seam and loose thread on each side.

8. To finish, stitch one hole backwards so the threads are the same side. Sew one of the threads back one hole and the other back two holes to lock the stitches in place so you don't have to made a knot, and trim the threads.

MEMORABLE MOMENTS

Susie: 'I just take my time, You never want to rush it.
You never want to feel the pressure of time.'

One man who fought in two world wars left a remarkable legacy, including a helmet, a pair of stirrups and a war diary outlining his exploits at the front.

Inevitably, time and active service had taken their toll. The worn steel helmet was missing a chin strap and one of the leather fastenings on the stirrups had snapped. However, even if the cover of the diary was now fragile, his spidery handwriting was still clear. For leather expert Suzie it was an opportunity to pay a personal tribute to a brave soldier whose voice could still be heard, by replacing and rejuvenating helmet and stirrups so they lasted another century at least.

Initially First World War soldiers fought in cloth caps, until the introduction of the bowl-shaped steel helmet in 1915, designed by John L Brodie and officially called Helmet, Steel, Mark I. Helmets weren't universally welcomed in the army until statistics proved their worth in protecting wearers from head injuries.

Given the dent in the top of the helmet, it seems fortunate this soldier had worn one. The treasured items were brought in by his grandson who explained that their owner had joined the army as a teenager in the First World War and seen action at Gallipoli, the Somme and then finally at Ypres.

One diary entry might explain how a ding occurred. 'On Friday we got very close to the firing line. Shells seemed to whizz a few inches above us and shrapnel burst close to where we were several times. One hit my helmet. A fellow said: "Are you all right?"'

After the conflict he was in the Territorial Army as a cavalryman and was pictured in the spurs as part of the official parade at the coronation of George VI. Two years later he was called up for service in the Second World War, surviving the carnage of Dunkirk.

The patina on the outside of the helmet was testament to the action it had seen so there were no plans to change it. But Suzie set about making a chin strap by cutting a strip of new leather of an appropriate length. To soften its sharpness she used an edging tool to pare down the angle. After staining the new leather to give it uniformity she ran it through cloth held in gloved hands, gradually introducing a new softness. Before threading it through the buckles on the helmet she heated a creasing iron to add a decorative trim. Inside the helmet, the lining of Rexine leather cloth was subjected to a careful clean using pipe cleaners to draw off the gathered dirt.

Suzie was determined to keep the same leather on the stirrups because, although it was dry and brittle, she could still sense some strength in it. Carefully she applied oils and grease until a little suppleness returned, then she could attach a backing.

To splice together the split in one of the straps she cut both sides into wedges, so one would slide alongside the next, and used adhesive to fix them. Although the repair would always represent a weakness, it meant the original leather could be preserved.

As she used fine wire wool to clean up the stirrups she discovered the name of the manufacturer, Moss Bros of Covent Garden, London. The extraordinary heirlooms that transformed one man into his grandson's boyhood hero were ready to inspire generations to come.

* * *

Once, a travelling man relied on a sturdy leather trunk to keep his possessions intact – and the most fortunate chose one made by Louis Vuitton.

So it was for one Victorian agricultural expert who travelled the globe with just such a trunk which, according to publicity, had 'unpickable locks' to help keep goods and clothing safe.

When his great grandson brought the trunk into The Repair Shop it was for leather expert Suzie to rejuvenate the dry, biscuity leather and undertake several repairs.

Trunks like this had wooden frames covered in 3mm-thick leather and were lined inside. Some were custom made, and travellers flung back the lids to reveal cupboards, cabinets or even an ironing board. Box maker Louis Vuitton began his company in Paris in 1854, with the first London branch opening some 30 years later.

There was no doubt about this case's provenance, with the prestigious name appearing on studs holding the leather in place. But when Suzie tried to free the stubs of a broken handle from the case she discovered the stud stalks were bent back and so impossible to move. Determined to re-use the monographed studs she was compelled to peel back a section of the linen lining to straighten them before they could be lifted out. It all created considerably more work but, as she observed, as someone had made the case in the first place so it could always be re-made. It was the order in which tasks were undertaken that was key.

The hinge that held the heavy lid in place had split so Suzie made another from new leather. She also cut a replacement over-strap, treading it into the gravel path outside before fixing it to the trunk to age it so it would better blend in. To feed the leather she used saddle soap, creating a lustre without masking any of the marks that were a memory of ships and trains during voyages of a bygone age.

USEFUL TERMS

Tensile strength: Each piece of leather has a tensile strength, the strain that can be applied to it before breaking.

Splitting: The hide is split into layers, with the top being a fine, smooth grain leather and the underside used for suede.

TEDDIES
AND TOYS

Toys are made to be treasured by their young owners, but sometimes they end up bearing the scars of being loved too much. Coupled with great age, the consequences of abundant affection bestowed over years can turn a once proud figure into something weary and worn.

This was the case with the elephant on wheels bought for Pam Edwards by her father when she was a toddler. Every Thursday afternoon the elephant went on parade, being ridden or dragged across the small Welsh town where she grew up to have tea with an auntie.

When it was presented to her, Pam – who had never seen an elephant before – cried: 'What a big mouse.' And after the elephant arrived at The Repair Shop it was promptly named Mouse by Amanda Middleditch and Julie Tatchell, known as 'The Bear Ladies' for their expertise in repairing vintage teddies and toys.

They had their work cut out with Mouse, who had no eyes or tusks and whose detached ears arrived separately in a bag. His accessories were frayed, his wheels were wobbly and there were bald patches starting to appear on his body. Constructed on a metal frame, they estimated that the toy was at least second-hand when it came to Pam as it was made in about 1910. The wood wool stuffing inside was disintegrating, causing the body and the legs to sag.

The first task was to painstakingly remove the accessories that had been glued to the toy's body years before. Not wanting to further damage the ageing fabric, it was a case of removing threads from the glue film one at a time. In doing so, they noticed different threads on the headdress, which once held bells in place, and the stubby felt foundations of the missing tusks.

Crude stitching attached the elephant's tail to its body. Often, Julie and Amanda choose to leave previous repairs in place as they form part of the toy's heritage. However, on this occasion the stitches had created a weak point on the elephant's backside that needed reinforcing if his tail was to be attached correctly.

With all the accessories and body parts removed, Mouse was vacuumed and gently washed to revive the flagging fur. Only when it was completely dry did they begin carefully reconstructing the toy. Its ears were added after being lined in red felt. Two vintage eyes taken from their collection helped to transform Mouse's hitherto blank expression and his trunk end was artfully renewed, not only lined with matching red felt but now clutching a hand-sewn peanut. After being lined with felt, worn patches on his body were darned so as to strengthen the vintage fabric.

Pure wool felt for the new saddle and headdress was chosen carefully in a muted scarlet, so as not to look too new and out of place, and sewn to the felt-lined back. Julie mimicked the decorative stitches that had graced the originals and two shiny bells were attached.

The job wasn't complete, though, until two other Repair Shop experts had played their part. Steve attached one of the rudimentary wooden wheels that had come loose, while Will waxed them, bringing up a protective shine that would ensure they kept rolling for many years to come.

Mouse was once again a picture of dignity and elegance and Pam was overwhelmed by his appearance. Although his fading glory was rejuvenated, he was instantly recognisable as the toy she knew and loved.

How to Age Your Bear

Since 1902, when American President Theodore Roosevelt lent his nickname, Teddy, to jointed toys made in the image of a bear, their popularity has never been dented. Today, they are made in quantity all over the world. But if you have kept a bear from childhood or are a keen collector, there are signs that point to which decade it was made in.

1900–1910

Morris Michtom created a soft toy in honour of the US President who, as a hunter, had become famous for refusing to shoot a tethered bear. Sales led to the launch of the Ideal Novelty & Toy Company in America. At the same time, the Steiff family in Germany were making long-limbed, slightly humped-back bears, with stringed joints quickly replaced by metal. From 1904, Steiff bears were distinctive for having a button sewn into an ear, a trademark that goes on until the present day. Buttons on vintage toys are often long gone, but check to see if there is a hole where one previously existed. Steiff toys, along with others, also bore chest and ear tags. The bodies of early bears were made from mohair and were stuffed with wood wool, which feels crunchy when it's squeezed. Black boot buttons or wooden buttons were used as eyes, while noses were sewn on. The pads of the bears were usually made out of felt.

1910–1920

Glass eyes were now the norm, while kapok, a natural fibre from the seed pod of a tropical tree, began to replace wood wool inside stuffed toys. Sometimes both substances were used. As a result, teddies were firmer and heavier. German makers Bing produced the first wind-up teddy bear in 1910. An all-black bear, representing national mourning, was sold in the aftermath of the *Titanic* disaster in 1912. Other toys also distinguished the era, with many being made from First World War coats, shirts or army blankets. German bears, distinctive for having long arms and snouts, were not imported into the UK during the conflict.

1920–1930

Artificial silk plush was now the fabric of choice for teddy bear makers and cotton was a popular fabric for paws. In 1921, author A. A. Milne bought a bear made by toy firm J. K. Farnell, which became the inspiration for Winnie-the-Pooh. Merrythought, a Shropshire-based company, began manufacturing a distinctive broad-headed, wide-eared bear.

1930–1940

Manufacturers developed unofficial trademarks, like sewing noses in a particular shape or colour. Nylon silk plush was invented in 1938 and the bears being made from it generally had flatter faces and shorter limbs.

1940–1950

An alternative toy filling used by makers during the Second World War was dubbed 'sub', effectively the sweepings from the mill floor. It feels denser and heavier that other stuffings. In 1945, Wendy Boston began making the first non-jointed bears. Three years later she included the earliest lock-in eyes to reflect increasing concerns about child safety. Koala bears made from kangaroo skin started appearing in homes, sent as gifts by distant relatives.

Foam rubber was now being used to fill an acrylic plush body, and by 1954, the first fully washable bear was produced, delighting housewives who could now regularly put washed and sodden toys through the mangle. Wendy Boston even ensured both ears and head were made from a single piece of material, so one wouldn't be lost when it was pegged on the line. Plastic became a mainstay of teddy bear features. Stitched noses were replaced with moulded plastic ones and glass eyes were likewise dispatched to history. Screw-in plastic eyes closely resembled their glass counterparts though. One way to distinguish which your bear has is to hold the eye to your lip. If it feels abnormally cold, it is glass, while if it is room temperature, it is made from plastic.

1960–1970

Teddy bears became ubiquitous, usually filled with polyester wadding. But there was a rival for the affections of the latest generation of children with the popularity of pandas, in the wake of Chi Chi the giant panda's arrival at London Zoo. If a bear or panda had joints, they were by now made from plastic. But safety laws were being tightened to stop them being removable or a choking hazard.

A Selection of Julie and Amanda's Workshop Tools

Working from a studio, Julie and Amanda have numerous crafting tools that assure them of professional results. However, perhaps the most valuable items, packed safely in plastic tubs, are the collection of vintage eyes gathered down the years that can restore the kindly character of an ancient teddy.

1. **Needles of all sizes:** From 25cm (10 inch) doll needles, long enough to pass through a doll's head when fixing eyes, all the way down to small needles with impossibly small eyes to thread.

2. **Needle-nose pliers**: Also known as pointy-nose, long-nose or snipe-nose pliers, these are needed to curl the pointed ends of the cotter pin joints, which are used to give soft toys moveable joints.

3. **Wooden handled stuffing sticks:** In various sizes, these are wielded through small seam openings to pack soft toy stuffing into bodies and limbs. Stuffing is wound around the prongs like candy floss and pressed in to achieve a firm finish.

4. **Brushes:** These help to care for the fur coats of much-loved toys. Julie and Amanda have a variety, including slicker brushes, like those used for pets, through to wire brushes. The choice of brush depends on the frailty of the material.

5. **Large headed pins:** These are used in toy-making so there's no danger of one getting left behind. Julie and Amanda have found rusty short pins inside soft toys left over from previous repair work.

6. **Good light:** Needed for close work like stitching and darning.

7. **Thread:** The correct thread helps to disguise a repair. Julie and Amanda use strong thread with a matt finish rather than a shiny alternative.

Our Favourite Tools

Every working day, no matter what job is in hand, Julie and Amanda reach for their small, sharp embroidery scissors to snip stitches or thread or even make small holes. Easily lost during busy days, scissors like this are vital for tackling delicate or fiddly tasks.

PROJECTS

HOW TO WASH YOUR BEAR

No matter how clean a home, bears kept on shelves and beds may well pick up dust or even acidic grit, which will penetrate the fur pile causing damage. Jointed or aged bears and toys can be washed, but it needs to be a careful operation.

1. Lightly brush and vacuum the bear.

2. Using a mild detergent, like baby shampoo, whip up suds and put only the bubbles on the bear.

3. Wring out a flannel and use it to remove the soap. Avoid scrubbing, wringing and rubbing.

4. Dry naturally, by sitting the bear on a towel in the airing cupboard. If the job has been done properly it should not be that wet.

5. If the toy is two-tone, like a panda, consider taking it apart for washing to avoid the risk of dyes bleeding from one area to the next.

6. Consider using insect-repelling cedar wood balls and lavender bags within your bear collection.

HOW TO MEND YOUR BEAR

Using skills they picked up at their grandmothers' knees, Julie and Amanda have made a thriving business out of bear repair. Just by looking at a beloved toy they can tell how it has been carried: by an ear if it's missing, by a limb if the stuffing is crushed, in the crook of an arm if the head has been pushed sideways. When paw pads are threadbare and noses have been kissed away, the pair pool their knowledge and skills and aim to restore a bear, or any other cuddly toy for that matter, so it can be handed to the next generation looking just as it always has. When it's a toy that has accompanied someone through childhood illness, wartime evacuation or any other given trauma, then repairs need the utmost care and, Julie and Amanda say, it's a privilege to undertake work on items of such great sentimental value. It's estimated a quarter of people keep their childhood companion into adulthood, although time inevitably takes its toll. Julie and Amanda happily tackle the tricky task of re-lining toys to help preserve vintage outer fabrics, using techniques honed through their careers. On particularly frail areas, they choose conservation netting to cover holes before darning. But some refurbishment is within many people's skill set. Here's their advice for anyone embarking on a bear repair.

1. First, buy a jointed soft toy from a charity shop and dismantle it, to better understand some of the pitfalls ahead. Or purchase a bear-making kit.

2. Before starting on your chosen toy, photograph it from all angles, so you have evidence of what it looked like before the repair process started.

3. Do some historical research to help preserve the toy's authenticity. Different manufacturers had hallmark habits, like the shapes of paws, the length of arm or the angle at which ears were attached, and these should be faithfully replicated.

4. Don't do anything you can't reverse. The aim is to ensure the bear resembles its original self.

5. Make sure all improvements are in keeping with the bear's character. For example, don't put a furry or new fabric arm on a balding body. That might mean reversing a piece of loom state mohair and pulling threads through from the back to make the new limb indistinguishable from the old.

6. Carefully colour-match new material with vintage. Julie and Amanda tone down the colours of modern fabrics by using mild dyes made from, amongst other things, diluted tea, coffee, turmeric and soot.

HOW TO STUFF A TEDDY BEAR
(OR OTHER SOFT TOY)

Keeping a favourite soft toy at its right weight regarding maintains its familiar expression and helps to preserve ageing fabric.

1. First locate the closing seam, which is usually stitched in a different way to the rest. In vintage bears it's likely to be hand-sewn and found along the back seam. On more modern soft toys the stitching will be overlocked and discreetly placed, for example, between the legs or on the back of the neck.

2. Carefully undo the closing seam using sharp embroidery scissors, without damaging the fabric.

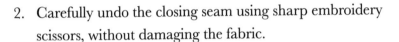

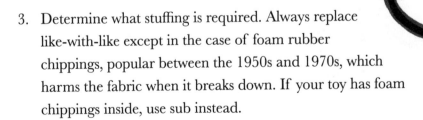

3. Determine what stuffing is required. Always replace like-with-like except in the case of foam rubber chippings, popular between the 1950s and 1970s, which harms the fabric when it breaks down. If your toy has foam chippings inside, use sub instead.

4. Always begin the process by stuffing the outer parts of the body, like the toes or muzzle.

5. Stuffing like sub or polyester should be 'fluffed' before being used. Julie and Amanda use a stuffing stick to pull it apart but a chopstick or spoon handle are also options.

6. Take small pieces of stuffing and place them inside the toy firmly and evenly, to avoid creating lumps.

7. Vintage fabrics are supported by appropriate depth of stuffing. Under-stuffing causes creases which stress the fibres and over stuffing generates unnecessary tension. Both could cause damage. Using memory and common sense, decide how firm your toy needs to be before neatly closing the seam once more.

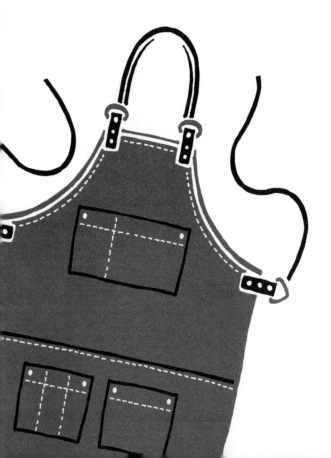

HOW TO RE-ATTACH A GLASS EYE

Bears of a certain age are distinguished by having glass eyes, attached in pairs. If time has taken its toll with one eye, it's likely the other will be failing soon, so take it off and fix both at the same time.

1. The glass eyes used with vintage or mohair bears have a wire loop in the back. Locate the original eye 'sockets', which will have flattened fur and a hole in the centre.

2. Pull a generous length of extra strong thread through the loop on the back of the replacement eye and double knot it so that the eye is held firmly in the centre of the thread.

3. Thread a long needle – known as a doll needle – with both ends of the thread and push the needle out towards the back of the head, so it emerges at the nape of the neck. (The needle needs to be longer than the depth of the head.)

4. Repeat steps 3–5 with the second eye, so the thread emerges at the same point.

5. Tie the eye threads firmly together at the back of the head, ensuring the tension is similar on each side.

6. Pass the remaining loose threads back through the bear's head and snip off any loose ends.

MEMORABLE MOMENTS

Julie: 'I get anxious before I reveal the item even though I know I have done my best. The relief I feel when I see the delight on the owner's face makes it all worthwhile.'

Amanda: 'I love working on the features of a bear, the face especially, all the things that give it character. I just love seeing them come back to life.'

Pink Teddy had an inspiring history. Bought for its owner during the Second World War from prestigious department store Harrods, it accompanied her when she was evacuated to Scotland and later, to boarding school. It was her companion during childhood illnesses and survived being played with by her children and grandchildren. Sadly, it didn't survive the attentions of a puppy.

Now minus one arm and half an ear, it arrived at The Repair Shop with an owner concerned that any repair work didn't bring about any loss in the dignity that befitted his senior years.

Rather than being made of mohair, this was a sheepskin bear, with mohair supplies at the time Pink Teddy was made being directed towards soldier's uniforms and blankets. But that meant the body was less durable than other bears. Julie and Amanda took enormous care as they snipped open a stomach seam and removed all the 'sub' used as stuffing.

To recreate the missing ear they took off Pink Teddy's remaining good one and split it. The original material then became the front of both ears while replacement fabric was put on the back.

When it came to disguising the new material on the back of the ears and the replacement arm Julie and Amanda had to recreate the pink tinge that the teddy's fur now bore. It turned out the best option in this case was hair dye, which was carefully applied to blend in with the rest of the body.

Although Pink Teddy looked just the same, it was benefitting from being lined which offered new resilience for future play. The owner didn't mind some distinguished bald patches. However, the repairers put on some almost invisible patches to ensure the body remained robust.

* * *

Beloved bears that suffer with the ravages of time are often subject to home repairs. George was one such bear, bought for the eldest of six daughters when she was born in 1941 and handed down through them all until being lovingly stitched by the youngest sister in a bid to stem damage.

The moment they saw George, Julie and Amanda recognised elements of his history. He was an Irish-made bear, common in Britain during the Second World War when the import of the more-ubiquitous German bears was halted. Typically Irish bears like George had ears riding high on heads which tended to be sharply triangular in shape and long limbs with pointy paws.

For now George's paws looked more stubby, after being turned over and sewed to stop stuffing leaking from worn-out pads. But the somewhat unsightly repair was welcomed by Julie and Amanda as it kept the original fabric intact.

Their first job was to empty George of stuffing. He was filled with wood wool, which gives a dry crunch when stuffed toys are squeezed. Using pliers the chest was emptied until they found the long-dead growler, once a memorable sound for its succession of owners.

With the paw pad beyond repair Julie and Amanda reversed all the limbs to sew in new felts ones from the inside. There was another new addition too, to make before the bear was re-assembled. The old growler couldn't be saved so it was replaced with a new one. Although it sounded more farmyard than wilderness, it was in fact a sound rooted in the noise a baby bear makes when calling for its mum.

After a missing eye was replaced, the last job of a pamper session fell to Julie. She massaged only the bubbles yielded by mild soap into his body before the foam was removed with a flannel. Afterwards he was dried and brushed, leaving him a smart ted ready to celebrate a fresh start as an octogenarian.

* * *

Throughout her childhood and beyond one woman held fast to her toy panda. It was a gift from her father who died when she was nine and afterwards, by her own admission, life went from colour to black and white. The loss haunted her for years during which time Panda become her only confidante and friend.

Fifty years later the English-made bear was suffering from bald patches, weak seams and missing facial features. The black fur was particularly worn, a problem Julie and Amanda have seen before and assume the dyeing process to be responsible.

First task for team was to remove the head, one small stitch at a time. Only then could the foam rubber stuffing be removed and the body parts separated before being cleaned, to avoid any risk of the dark colour leaching into the pale.

Each bit was then lined to give the ageing fabric new strength. When it came to sewing them back together Julie and Amanda were careful to follow pre-existing stitch lines. Fabric that had been hidden behind the seams for decades had vibrant colouring compared to the rest. But to give panda stripes to mark his age like this would mar his appearance. His label, originally sewn in upside down by the manufacturers, was also stitched back in exactly the same way.

Once the head was firm with new stuffing Amanda sewed on a new nose and replacement red tongue. She also had the tricky job of stitching the head back into place. Vintage fabrics are prone to stretching which could leave the bear with a drooping head or a cricked neck if the seams are inexpertly joined. Lining the fabric lends stability and that's how Julie and Amanda sidestepped the pitfall.

When he was returned to the owner, ready for a second lease of life, she felt the final piece in the bereavement puzzle had slotted into place.

USEFUL TERMS

Plush: A rich fabric of silk, cotton, wool or alpaca with a long, soft nap.

Mohair: The silky wool of an angora goat.

Squidge test: Not a textbook term, but one used by Julie and Amanda as they determine what the stuffing inside a bear is made from and whether it is disintegrating.

Arctophile: A teddy bear collector.

A hug of bears: The collective name for teddy bears.

Julie and Amanda's List of Do's and Don'ts

- *Do cuddle them regularly and, while doing so, check for signs of moth or carpet beetle damage. Both insects lay eggs inside toys and have larvae that feed on fabric, leaving bald patches and holes.*

- *Don't ignore early warning signs. If you suspect there are insects at large in your soft toy collection, put affected articles into a sealed plastic bag and pop them in a domestic freezer for two weeks. That's how long it will take to kill dormant eggs.*

- *Do take the vacuum on a low or upholstery setting to your soft toy to help deter infestations. Also, regular use of an appropriate brush is at the heart of a good maintenance routine.*

- *Don't keep soft toys in direct sunlight or next to radiators as heat may cause fabric deterioration.*

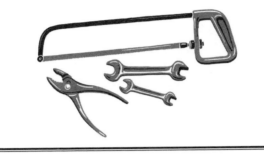

METALWORK

On Christmas morning in 1959, Mervyn Bell awoke to find a gleaming red go-kart waiting for him under the tree. Nearly sixty years later, the go-kart had wobbly wheels, a holed seat and its paintwork bore multiple scars. All the signs were that the low-slung vehicle had been ridden exhaustively by Mervyn and, much later, his children. Now it was time for grandchildren to enjoy this much-loved machine – but not before The Repair Shop's resident metalworker Dominic Chinea made it roadworthy once more.

Made by toy company Tri-ang, the design of this three-wheeled go-kart was striking. Riders pulled two upright handles forwards and backwards to operate cranks that turned the wheels, so heading up hill needed strong arms rather than legs. Their feet rested on a bar that linked the two front wheels and steered by pushing one foot or the other forward.

Tri-ang – part of the world's biggest toy company in the middle of the twentieth century – also made bicycles and pedal cars, marketing their products as 'the toys for happy and healthy recreation'.

Metalworker Dom's first task was to take the go-kart apart and give it a thorough clean, assessing each piece individually before deciding on his next move. With the original red paint hidden by a coat of black, he was at first reluctantly resigned to a re-spray. But now some vigorous rubbing removed the black, so Dom re-evaluated. After some considered touching up with carefully matched paint, the metalwork matched the fifties finish once more, although selected dings and dents gathered over the years were deliberately left in evidence, as reminders of Mervyn's childhood scrapes.

Although the larger rear wheel was original, the two front ones had already been replaced by smaller versions of those initially used, making the front dip and posing a problem that even the power of the internet couldn't solve. While Tri-ang was a well-known toy manufacturer, this particular go-kart model was unusual and *The Repair Shop* research team, along with Dom, struggled to find any original images for comparison purposes. Finally, he settled on a pair of wheels from a similarly aged Tri-ang pram. At the time manufacturers used the same fittings across different ranges, so there was no need to modify the go-kart to fit the new wheels. At the back the wheel was in poor condition, with loose spokes in danger of buckling. Bicycle expert Tim Gunn, working alongside Dom at The Repair Shop, replaced the spokes and put on a new solid rubber tyre.

To make the seat serviceable again, the rusted hole in the metal saddle was cut out and patched up, and a new mounting point for it was welded in too. Once again, when thoroughly cleaned the saddle had ample amounts of the original green paint, which Dom was able to colour-match so it was fully refurbished.

There was evidence that the manufacturer's sticker had once been on the framework, but sourcing an authentic replacement proved impossible. Instead, Dom took a digital copy of a time-appropriate sticker and made one himself, even fashioning some symptoms of wear and tear.

With the go-kart in bits on his work bench, Dom likened it to a giant Meccano set. When it was back in one piece again, after some careful handling to avoid scratching the paintwork, Mervyn was transported back to his childhood, while his grandchildren were transported up some nearby Tarmac, after seizing the chance to try it out.

TYPES OF METAL

When he works with metal, Dominic is continuing a tradition forged in ancient times, when the earliest chemists experimented with ores found in the Earth's crust.

Smelting copper with tin created bronze, a more durable metal than anything else available at the time. This distanced civilisations in command of bronze-making technology from their Stone Age predecessors, giving them stronger tools and weapons, and a desirable commodity to trade.

The Bronze Age, which lasted for centuries, was itself superseded by an age when iron predominated. Both are broad-brushstroke terms, as their dates were dictated as much by geographic location as the calendar. Iron had a much higher melting point than either copper or tin. A shortage of tin in about 1,300 BC prompted a leap forward in iron smelting, which produced cheaper, more durable ironware. Other metals known in antiquity were gold, silver, lead and mercury. Nickel and chromium were discovered in the eighteenth century, aluminium in the nineteenth century, while plutonium was among 20 metals found in the twentieth century.

Today, there are more than 80 metals recorded on the periodic table, the names of most being unfamiliar to us. However, they share a few common properties with the metals and alloys we know well. Metals are shiny, good conductors of heat and electricity, and have a high melting point. They are ductile or pliable when put under stress, hence their use in cabling, and sonorous or resonant when they are struck, thus are made into church bells.

Here's a quick guide to common metals:

Aluminium: Soft, lightweight and fireproof, it brings these qualities to any alloy. In a raw state, it is found in the ground as abundant bauxite.

Iron: Pure iron is silvery-white in colour and almost soft enough to cut with a knife. To become a functional metal it is treated in a blast furnace and adopts numerous forms, including cast iron, when molten iron is poured into a mould and allowed to cool, and wrought iron, when liquid iron is mixed with some of the waste products in production. Basic raw iron is called pig iron.

Steel: Pig iron is the major component of steel, which is then mixed with other metals to form a broad range, each with particular strengths. For example, pig iron blended with chromium and nickel creates stainless steel, famously resistant to corrosion, while pig iron with tungsten and nickel makes tool steel, which is then toughened by a tempering process. Although there are scores of different steels, the greatest made by volume is carbon steel.

Chromium: Best known as a shiny car part, chromium is tough and lustrous. As an alloy with cobalt and tungsten it makes Stellite, which is used for cutting tools.

Copper: Versatile copper, mined throughout the world, can be found in anything from cooking pans to the Statue of Liberty. Copper and zinc together produce brass.

Tin: A silvery-white metal produced by smelting the ore cassiterite. Food tins are coated with tin to stop the steel beneath from rusting or reacting with the contents.

A Selection of Dom's Workshop Tools

As a professional metalworker – as well as restoration projects he's also a set designer – Dom has machinery at hand that most people wouldn't recognise, let alone use. But he also owns a large range of tools that are more familiar, which he's been collecting since the age of 14.

1. **Large collection of hammers with heads bearing different contours:** Dom uses these for panel beating.

2. **Clamps:** These lend a firm grip when items are being welded together.

3. **Shaped dollies, spanners, pliers and metal saws:** All these feature in his range of hand tools.

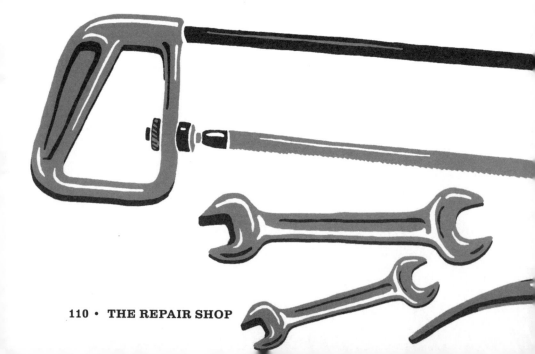

4. **Angle grinder:** With its various attachments, it can be a cleaner or a cutter.

5. **Welders:** Dom has two: a Mig welder, used to weld steel, and a Tig welder, a much more adaptable machine used for aluminium, stainless steel, even brass or copper.

My Favourite Tools

A collection of metal engineering set squares take pride of place in Dom's workshop. Ranging in size from 2cm (¾ inch) to 62cm (24½ inches), he uses them to mark straight lines and accurate angles.

Projects

HOW TO DEAL WITH RUST

1. If an old tool hasn't been used for a long time and has seized up, soak it in a mix of acetone and automatic transmission fluid for a few days to free up the internal mechanism.

2. With a small rusty item, like a tool, leave it to soak in white vinegar to kick-start the de-rusting process.

3. Afterwards, use a pad of wire wool in conjunction with a lubricating oil to tackle the rust that's still clinging to it. Wire wool comes in numerous different grades, with 4 being coarse and 0000 super fine. It's advisable to start with a fine mesh and graduate upwards.

4. If the rust remains stubborn, there are further options, ranging from a nylon-bristled toothbrush, through brass and steel brushes to an angle-grinder attachment.

5. With chrome, use one of the least abrasive wire wools with lubricating oil. The presence of rust indicates the chrome plating has broken down, revealing the steel below. In order to stem rust for good it needs to be professionally re-plated, but you can delay that by putting on a protective coat of wax.

HOW TO ELIMINATE A MARK
ON NEWLY PAINTED METAL

A fly corpse or a running drip ruins an otherwise unbroken sheen on a recently painted metal item, but the problem is soon remedied.

1. Use a face mask to protect against dust.

2. Take what's known as wet and dry sandpaper, that is, very fine sandpaper. To work out what you need, look for the number on the label. The lower the number, the rougher the grit. So 30 grit is very coarse, 100 grit is medium and 320 grit is fine. But this is a job for a sandpaper classified as more than 2,000 grit.

3. Use the sandpaper with a bucket of water containing a few drops of washing-up liquid, washing the sandpaper out frequently in the water.

4. Using a sanding block to keep everything flat, rub over the imperfections. That should be sufficient to take off the top layer of paint without leaving scratch marks.

5. Polish to perfect the finish.

MEMORABLE MOMENTS

Dom: 'There are so many things going on inside my head when I see a new project; the thought process begins immediately, starting with what's needed, drawing up a plan of attack and the end goal that I'm trying to achieve. And also, I must make sure it is safe.'

In the 1930s Manchester and nearby towns were criss-crossed with 470 km (292 miles) of tramlines and 953 trams trundled along 46 different routes daily. Among the 328 million passengers each year was a schoolgirl who saved up her pocket money for the sheer joy of riding the number 81 service between Salford and Deansgate.

But after operating costs soared and tracks were ripped up for the war effort, its days were numbered. The trams were shut down in 1947 and a vast number of carriages were dispatched into a mammoth bonfire. Although she was devastated by the closure, the schoolgirl who loved riding the trams enjoyed a stroke of luck as her parents' neighbour brought back a tram seat which took pride of place in the family's front garden. Later her widowed mum sat in it, chatting to neighbours and passers-by.

Wooden tram seats sat in an iron framework and were distinguished from others by a slot on the seat side that enabled the back rest to be pushed to and fro, so passengers could face the direction of travel.

Seventy years, on the seat had suffered in the face of British weather, and parts of it had already been inexpertly renewed.

Now aged 93, that schoolgirl was concerned her little piece of history was crumbling.

At The Repair Shop, Dom quickly realised it wasn't a case of rubbing down flaking paint and rust to secure this restoration. Much of the wood was rotting and the metalwork rusty. To make it structurally solid again would be a big task.

He began by dismantling the seat, making a careful plan of it as he went, and sending the metalwork off to be sandblasted. Before it was whisked away he spotted a tiny section bearing the original red coachwork, which he could then duplicate. With sections of wood shearing away, he decided to replace all the planks that formed the seat, together with the tricky-to-mimic curved side slots, using a chunky length of slow-growing American pitch pine, something similar to the material that would have been used for the original seats. Careful measuring meant he got all the necessary lengths from just one piece.

When he had the gentle lines of the new wooden seat in front of him, the sandblasted metalwork arrived back, giving him a new, unscheduled task. The process had been so robust it had stripped back more crumbling metal than expected. For safety reasons, he would have to copy its outline and cut a replica. Originally the frames would have been made in vast numbers, in a factory. Dom sought to imitate the curved feet by making relief cuts in the end metal section, and heat-treating it before bending it into shape. As a nostalgic reminder of the long lost travel system he painted the number 81 on the back rest, the last remaining piece of original wood. When it was re-assembled it looked just as it had when it was new, probably around the turn of the twentieth century. On this occasion it wasn't the attention to detail that gave Dom most job satisfaction but the elation of the owner, transported back to her youth thanks to his expertise.

* * *

Years before the advent of the internet, towns relied on signage to promote themselves and their wares, and a museum in Polperro, south east Cornwall, boasted an eye-catching board to attract visitors. It not only had large lettering and jangling bells but stood on a pole attached to a wheeled stand so it could be pushed around the thronging harbourside.

The fishing and smuggling museum was 'the place to see' in Polperro, it promised, although the sign itself had been smuggled out of the town at some stage. After being reclaimed from an antiques centre in Wales by a resident, the community now needed this uncommon placard, set in its wrought iron frame, future-proofed so it could rally tourists once more around the town's narrow streets.

Fortunately, metalworker Dom was given a decades-old postcard featuring the curiosity in its prime before damp sea air had beckoned in the rust.

To rid the sign of rust – essential if it was to survive for further decades – he had to rub down both the sign and the frame. It meant erasing the remainder of the lettering but Dom set about tracing what was left to preserve the size and style beforehand. With a clean slate he could re-paint the white background and re-draw the black lettering in durable sign-writing paint in the same style as the original.

The links that held the bells in place were worn thin and needed replacing while the bells themselves were tarnished. At this point Steve Fletcher offered to dip the brass bells in clock cleaning fluid to help bring back their shine.

Jay was also recruited onto the project, to replace long colourful tassles that had once hung down the sides of the frame. Making the most of the internet himself, he took tuition tips from a nine-year-old before setting about making them himself.

After replacing frail and eroded metal curls, Dom cleaned, primed and painted the framework in red, yellow and blue. The two dozen bells were re-attached along with the tassels and it was ready to face time and tide in the Cornish fishing village once again.

USEFUL TERMS

Coated abrasives: The proper name for sandpaper.

Oily rag restoration: A term used when restoring an item, but preserving as much of the original patina as possible. Rubbing a lightly oiled cloth over the metal item helps protect it from further encroachment by rust.

Steel wool: Another term for wire wool.

Dom's List of Do's and Don'ts

Although the specialist equipment necessary for major metalwork projects is beyond ordinary householders, some items can still be stripped down at home. Here Dom signposts the best way forward.

- *Do take photographs, measurements and even drawings of your item before you begin a refurbishment project. Document everything that might help when it comes to re-assembly.*

- *Don't forget to use protective gear and clothing.*

- *Do label everything as you take items apart. Put screws in named bags, for example, and use paper tags on larger items to avoid confusion in the future.*

- *Don't use the wrong type of paint. For example, restored items staying outdoors need the protection of exterior paint and will deteriorate without it.*

- *Do think outside the box when you undertake repairs and use different component parts, if necessary. When Dom fixed a spinning barber's pole, he discovered the manufacturers used a motor from a gramophone.*

- *Don't skimp on preparation. Procedures like cleaning and sanding down may seem tediously repetitive, but any compromises taken here will be visible in the end result.*

- *Don't use excess paint in the hope of hiding areas that haven't been properly prepared. Layers of shiny paint will only amplify any outstanding issues.*

- *Do create a template out of cardboard or even wood if you are making or designing a new part for an item, to be sure your planned addition will fit.*

- *Don't strive for perfection at all costs. The quest for a flawless replica is daunting and deters many from starting a project.*

- *Do become a hoarder. Dom buys inexpensive broken items at sales to liberate unusual nuts and bolts and other mechanical debris that he may well need for future restorations.*

- *Do use the correct drill bits for the job as those designed for masonry will make a mess of metal. Everything is easier with the right tool!*

UPHOLSTERY

After it opened in 1914, Derby Hippodrome was an elegant variety theatre, packed to capacity each week as it hosted the nation's best-loved acts. Later it became a cinema and its final incarnation before closure in 2006 was as a bingo hall.

Seat number 11 from the now defunct building found its way to The Repair Shop after Jamie Woods liberated it from his parents' attic. It had long been a fixture there after plans to renovate it were shelved, with bingo cards lying unnoticed in the wooden pocket on the chair back. The well-worn flip-up seat chair, had only one arm rest and arrived in pieces, with the metal framework that formed its sides also missing the base necessary for it to be freestanding.

It was the first time upholstery expert Sonnaz Nooranvary had renovated a folding theatre chair and she began by stripping back the threadbare green velvet that gave a nod to its former glory, levering out traditional pins that clung stubbornly to the frame.

Inside she found the coiled springs that gave the seat its bounce in such good condition that they could be re-used. Nestling among them she found a tell-tale label, revealing the seat was originally the work of the Elson & Robbins Company, experts in sprung units, based in Long Eaton, Nottinghamshire, which was the heart of the UK's furniture industry in the early twentieth century.

Carefully poking the label back into place, she replaced the ageing hessian that covered the springs with new, stapling it into place around the wooden seat base. Then she stitched the springs firmly to the hessian across the seat to stop them slipping out of position. On the top she added two layers of foam to create extra comfort, using contact adhesive to bond them all into a single unit.

As she turned her attention to the seat covering, metalworker Dom Chinea was rubbing down and re-painting the metal frame in a warm gold and fashioning a replacement arm rest, as well as new 'feet' that would make it a stand-alone item at last. Sonnaz had identified a richly textured green velvet as a replacement fabric, slightly brighter than the original, but in a tone reminiscent of its theatre heyday.

Before measuring, she checked the direction of the fabric pile so that when fixed into place, it ran from top to bottom and from back to front. That meant sitting in the chair wouldn't entail an uncomfortable conflict between clothes and pile.

On the domed seat base she used staples to secure the plush material into position, while on the back she chose more traditional tacks around the edges, for aesthetic purposes, trapping a shallow piece of foam into place. Once that was completed, she could re-assemble the chair in preparation for Jamie's arrival. While to him it appeared almost new, the marks on the surviving arm rest told a different story, scored or scuffed by countless thousands of snugly seated theatre-goers, as they cheered and chortled down the decades.

HALLMARKS OF THE ERA

The craft of upholstery in Britain dates back at least to the fifteenth century, when a guild began. But upholders, as they were called, didn't make squashy sofas and soft chairs; rather they created curtains, drapes, tapestries – all vital for insulation – and lined coffins.

At that time furniture was rigidly unforgiving as bare wood was the sole option, with the only relief for the numb backsides sitting on them coming in the form of an animal skin. Only when cushions started being made in the Middle Ages – from leather and stuffed with dried palm leaves – was there some respite.

By the time Queen Elizabeth I was on the throne, padded chairs began to proliferate, partly because the art of stitched edging was developed. For the first time, furniture makers could stuff sawdust, grass, feathers or deer, goat and horse hair into a chair cover to create a luxury seat, albeit still hard.

After the influence of the Puritans ebbed away, the first daybeds were designed, the ancestors of today's sofas, and makers began to decorate exposed parts of the wooden frames. Still, furniture like this really was the preserve of the very rich until Victorian times, when there were two important innovations. Firstly, there was the helical or coiled steel spring, invented just before Victoria arrived on the throne, that kept its shape in a seat pad providing it was adequately lashed into place to control the way it compressed. Then came an abundant supply of fabric being produced in the factories spawned by the Industrial Revolution. Cotton wastage from the burgeoning factories, dubbed mill puff, was used for stuffing.

With a soft furnishings industry in full swing, there were initially chairs stuffed with coir, taken from coconuts, and alva marina, a seaweed found in France and on the Baltic Coast. But after the Germans pioneered the use of curled horse hair – the tail and mane of the animal – its popularity put other choices in the shade and it endured throughout Europe. At the time it was far cheaper to come by as horses were used for transport. Now a more expensive option, it is nonetheless a matter of etiquette to replace horse hair stuffing when older items are re-upholstered today. As manufacturers competed in the comfort stakes, sofas and chairs became increasingly plump, until buttoning and deep buttoning became fashionable.

Duck, goose and swan feathers provided another source of stuffing, especially for cushions and top-of-the-range furniture. Milled or chopped feathers were a lesser product.

Foam rubber, first developed in the twenties, became widely used in upholstery after the Second World War.

A SELECTION OF SONNAZ'S UPHOLSTERY TOOLS

Sonnaz is another of The Repair Shop experts who generally favour second-hand tools for the workshop above new, in terms of quality and longevity.

1. **Regulator:** With two ends – one pointed and the other flat – the regulator is essential when it comes to renovation. The pointed end is designed to tease out horse-hair stuffing, bringing about a smoother finish in old-style seating, while the flat end is useful in pleating when buttons are added.

2. **Tack hammer:** To knock in the pins that hold material in place.

3. **Staple gun:** Staples are used in quantity to secure hessians and fabrics to seat frames.

4. **Rulers:** Essential for measuring out material.

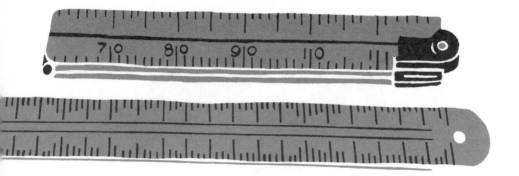

5. **Bull-nosed pliers:** For gripping and pulling out staples.

6. **Tack lifters:** Used to remove historic upholstery pins.

7. **Chalk or wax:** Both are used to mark up material before cutting.

8. **Hot melt glue gun:** Electrically powered so the glue – inserted in stick form – is heated as it comes out of a nozzle, to allow maximum dexterity in tasks like attaching braid.

My Favourite Tools

With cutting material a key part of her job, Sonnaz values above all a pair of shears that are sharp from hilt to tip. Although sometimes the term is interchangeable with scissors, shears are typically longer and heavier in the hand and leave a crisp edge.

Projects

HOW TO REPLACE DECORATIVE BRAID THAT'S PEELING OFF

Sometimes it's the little things that need fixing. Replacing the decorative edge on an ageing chair is often sufficient to give it a fresh look.

1. Measure the length of braid already in position before buying its replacement.

2. Gently remove the failing braid.

3. Fold the new braid's raw end under and track a hot melt glue gun along the line left by the previous one. With careful manipulation you should be able to achieve a perfect curve, but there are obviously perils to using a glue gun like this without considerable practice.

4. For beginners, try instead folding the end over and use coloured tacks to fix the braid in place. After putting the first tack in place, put some tension into the braid by pulling it before inserting the next tack some 10cm (4 inches) from the first. It's likely this will result in a '50 pence piece' effect around the top of a chair.

5. Finish by folding over the fraying edge of the braid back beneath itself and fix it in place with a tack.

HOW TO REPLACE THE COVER OF A DROP IN DINING CHAIR SEAT

The patina gathered on wooden tables and chairs are attractive signs of age and the joys of meals past. But the material covers on seats are prone to altogether less appealing bald patches. Happily, these can be swiftly rejuvenated by anyone confident in cutting material and using a staple gun.

1. Take the seat out of the dining chair and carefully remove all the staples holding the fabric in place.

2. Take off the 'bottom cloth', the mono-coloured material beneath the seat that hides the chair seat's insides.

3. Using the old cover as a template, mark out a replacement for both from new material using chalk or wax.

4. Check that you have the measurements right.

5. Using sharp shears, cut out the new material.

6. Lay the seat material centrally on the pad, then flip it over so the bottom of the seat is facing you.

7. Find the centre of one of the sides and staple the material in place. Repeat for the other three sides, being careful to maintain a tension in the fabric as you do so.

8. Now staple along the remainder of the sides to the corners. Be sure the fabric remains stretched or there's a risk that the seat will look saggy.

9. Fold the corners into a neat pleat and staple. There should be evidence on the original piece of material about how this was first done, which might help.

10. Take the replacement bottom cloth – usually hessian or black Diprol – and fold over the raw edges before stapling it into position.

HOW TO MAKE SCATTER CUSHIONS

Cushions can add opulence, colour and comfort to any space, no matter how small, and they are simple to make, especially if you have access to a sewing machine.

1. If you plan to make 45cm (18 inch) cushions, cut out two 50cm (20 inch) squares with careful use of a rule and chalk.

2. Turn the right sides of the material to face each other.

3. Choose a point about 15 cm (6 inches) from a corner to anchor your thread and sew towards the nearest corner.

4. Sew around the three other sides and about 15cm (6 inches) of the first side, leaving a gap of some 20cm (8 inches) in the centre.

5. Turn the cushion cover the right way around.

6. Choose your cushion filler. If you are using a hollowfibre pad, make sure it measures about 5cm (2 inches) more than the cushion cover. If it's feather, look for a cushion that's 10cm (4 inches) bigger, as these will compress more quickly over time.

7. Using a neat slip stitch, sew up the opening.

HOW TO REPLENISH THE STUFFING
IN A SOFA SEAT CUSHION

Over time, sofas start to sag as the stuffing inside is pummelled flat. This is a quick way to breathe new life into an old suite.

1. Buy some hollowfibre stuffing from a craft store – you may well use more than you think.

2. Take the cushion cover off.

3. Inside there will be another cover, this time made of calico or another utilitarian fabric that holds the stuffing in place. Unpick a portion of one of the back seams.

4. Push the stuffing into the cushion, taking care to space it evenly across the seat. Some cushions will have channels running down the seats that can be filled.

5. When the cushions look plump, sew up the opening with blanket stitch and replace the cover.

MEMORABLE MOMENTS

Sonnaz: 'I get real sense of freedom when I'm working with my hands and I love seeing things come together in front of my eyes. There is a magic that happens, especially when you are doing something for someone who you know will appreciate every detail you consider for them. It is amazing to think that many a craftsperson before me has stood at their bench doing what I am doing. It is fabulous to carry those skills forward.'

A sturdy chair was already a half century old when it was transported to Britain from Germany as a Jewish family fled from Nazi persecution. It was a chair associated with a beloved matriarch who saw her life turned upside-down after political upheaval in Europe.

As a child her great grand daughter plaited the fringe that encased its bottom edge and bounced on its broad seat. Now there was wear on the arms, a split in the seat and springs that were skew. Yet the chair's dark blue fabric was reinforced with squares of carpet, an upholstery technique that expert Sonnaz had never seen before. When she began stripping back the faded material, it seemed they were used as part of a repair. In any event, both colourful carpet sections were part of the furniture's familiarity and the owner wanted to keep them.

Wearing a mask to defend herself against a century and a half of gathered dust, she removed the old upholstery, revealing the original colour of the chair fabric as she did so. Jay used it to match some new material for the covers while Sonnaz retrieved the best preserved portion to make a scatter cushion.

Her first job on the chair was installing the webbing, the strips that support the body weight, which she stapled into place to get a firm grip in the ageing chair frame. Then she put in new springs which she lashed to keep them in place. After putting a layer of cotton felt on the seat for comfort she covered everything in a tight layer of calico, to hold everything firmly.

Still, Sonnaz was pondering the real purpose of the carpet pieces. She spent some of her childhood in Iran, the home of Persian rugs, and still had never seen a soft furnishings configuration like this one. As it happened, art conservator Lucia Scalisi, who had been observing the project from across The Repair Shop, had the answer.

The carpeting was in fact the split sides of a saddlebag, once used on a horse or camel and would have been decorated with the fringe that bedecked the bottom of the chair which colour-matched the squares perfectly. From clues in the pattern, it seemed the saddlebag was made in the second half of the nineteenth century in Shiraz, Iran. After Sonnaz stitched the saddlebag bag into place she shared her information with the owner, who had no idea of its provenance.

Clearly, the forced move from Germany was only half of the chair's story while its link to Iran would likely never be known.

* * *

The torn baize of a collapsible card table dating from the 1940s was marked with teacup rings and the imprint of a Worcestershire sauce bottle. If the table was to come into use again, the material would have to be replaced.

Yet Sonnaz and Will Kirk, who paired up to fix the table, were reluctant to bin the baize as it was a tangible link for one man to his grandfather. Not only did the older man used to eat at the table but he had his grandsons gather around it as together they worked out forthcoming match results in the hope of winning big on the weekly football pools. A family man, he didn't necessarily have money to spend on the youngsters but devoted ample amounts of time to them.

Biaze is a woollen fabric that's been made in England since 1783, making it one of the country's oldest fabrics. Apart from card tables it's been used for soundproofing, altar cloths and monks' habits.

The baize-covered section of the table could be liberated from the frame. One side of it was green, the other red. Sonnaz used shears to cut out the baize that remained, exposing the bare wood beneath. After stapling new fabric to the insert top and bottom, Sonnaz turned her talents to making coasters and a mat out of the redundant sections.

Will cleaned the corners of the table out before gluing and clamping them, to stop a previously persistent wobble. He also polished up the wooden legs. Now it was a table the owner hoped would become a living room memory for his own grandchildren.

USEFUL TERMS

Lashing springs: Tying springs into place so the load is equally spread.

Gimp pins: Fine, coloured tacks.

Webbing: Closely woven fabric strips for supporting the seats of upholstered chairs.

Deck: The flat platform under a seat cushion but above the springs, usually in plain material.

Ragtacker: The colloquial name for a journeyman upholsterer.

Sonnaz's List of Do's and Don'ts

- *Do measure twice or three times before cutting material, to help eliminate costly errors.*

- *Don't use blunt shears to cut material.*

- *Do take time. If something isn't going right, walk away and come back the next day when the answer to the problem will probably fall into place.*

- *Don't skimp on quality. From springs to stuffing, buy the best on offer in order to get great results. For example, hessian comes in two weights: 10oz (283g) and 12oz (340g). Always use the heavy weight option for upholstery.*

- *Do go the extra mile with fine detail.*

- *Don't assume you know everything. Always be open to learning new things, especially from people who've mastered the craft over decades.*

- *Do think about customising cushions, curtains or duvet covers by adding fringes, pompoms, braid or tassels.*

CERAMICS

In a fleeting moment, family heirlooms that have been cherished over several lifetimes can be reduced to shards. Many of us know that sinking feeling, as a sickening crash fills our ears, while cold dread clasps our hearts.

So it was for Norman Jenner, whose misplaced foot descending a ladder in his lounge started a domino effect that ended with a nineteenth century blue-and-white pitcher lying in pieces on the floor.

The statuesque ceramic once belonged to wife Brenda's grandmother. An impressive nineteenth century commemorative piece, its sides were busy with depictions of warriors in battle and were a source of endless fascination for Brenda as a child. She didn't know it then, but these were scenes from an historic massacre at Teutoburg Forest in Germany in 9 AD, when Roman soldiers were defeated by Germanic fighters and 35,000 legionnaires died.

Brenda finally inherited it after the death of her mother and it took pride of place in a bay window of her home before it toppled . After keeping the body of the pitcher and assorted remnants in a box for 15 years, the couple visited The Repair Shop to seek help from ceramics expert Kirsten Ramsay.

For her, commonplace domestic disasters like this one are meat and drink. Her first concern is always that as many broken pieces as possible are collected up and kept before they disappear up a vacuum. Happily, the Jenners had collected all the large pieces and many of the smaller ones. Then she must assess what she has – and what is missing – by fitting the fragments together like a 3-D jigsaw puzzle, feeling for that perfect fit to indicate the piece has found its proper home. Using tape to keep the pieces in place, she can start to picture an end result.

As she looked over the pitcher pieces, she discovered that Norman's mishap was not the first it had suffered. Yellowing glue clearly visible on the inside betrayed a previous breakage with a less-than-professional repair. It meant Kirsten had to remove all the old adhesive, by wielding a sharp scalpel, creating for herself several more pieces to fix.

Her next job was to remove dust and grime gathered on the glaze of the 120cm (47 inch) tall pitcher using a steam cleaner. It's a satisfying job, and also an ideal opportunity to put the item under close scrutiny, getting acquainted with its smallest details. In the frantic action played out on the pitcher, she saw raised swords, rearing horses and numerous silent screams in addition to the flowing scrollwork that bordered the terrifying tableau. And then she noticed a further crack in the body of the jug, caused during the firing process at the time it was made. It was a raised ridge rather than a rupture and had previously been filled with a rudimentary substance like plaster.

Before tackling that, she did a second dummy run with the broken pieces, this time scheduling the order in which she would glue them. There's no room for guesswork at this point. Without a system it's easy to bond four pieces in place and consequently find a fifth locked out. Using epoxy resin, she finally secured the pieces, once again using tape to hold them in position while the adhesive cured.

The job was far from complete, however. Often Kirsten would not repair a firing crack as it forms part of an item's heritage. But this was a large crack down the side of a big ceramic, so she chose to work on it to improve its stability. After removing the material that had been used previously to fill the firing crack, she mixed a two-part adhesive with various pigments to recreate the blue colour and unobtrusively pack the hairline fracture that remained. To plug gaps created by missing pieces, she used modelling clay mimicking the raised patterns evident on the original.

At last it was time to put the finishing touches to the pitcher and return it to its former glory. This entailed artful use of carefully mixed paints. The electric lights of The Repair Shop barn reflecting against the pitcher's shiny glaze made colour matching difficult, so Kirsten took the jug outside to complete the work in daylight.

When Brenda and Norman returned, they were stunned by the seamless repair, with the pitcher looking just as it had years before in Brenda's childhood. For them, it was like bringing a member of the family home. Through her painstaking observation, detailed attention and patience, Kirsten liberated this crushed pot from the attic and readied it for the next three generations.

TYPES OF CERAMICS

Ceramics is an umbrella term that covers a multitude of pieces that are shaped, decorated, glazed and fired. Remnants from ancient times reveal that ceramics have been part of human existence across the globe for millennia. In the earliest examples, clay was baked on a bonfire or left to dry in the sun. However, clay artefacts remained porous until the use of protective glaze spread from Egypt from the first century BC. Although terms related to ceramic items are commonly used interchangeably, there are defining traits to each.

Porcelain: This was first developed in China in about AD 600, when white kaolin clay was mixed with the mineral feldspar and quartz and fired at a high temperature. Its surface was translucent and smooth and it became the envy of trading nations everywhere. Inferior imitations of porcelain were made in Europe prior to the first decade of the eighteenth century, but lacked its hardness, translucency and colour. It was in Meissen, Germany, that the first proper European porcelain was then made, with French and British manufacturers soon adapting the recipe for themselves. Today, porcelain is fired at about 1,455 degrees Celsius (2,650 degrees Fahrenheit).

Fine china: The name given to European-made porcelain-style items, by way of recognition of the country where the porcelain tradition began. It's fired at 1,200 degrees Celsius (2,200 degrees Fahrenheit), making it softer than porcelain and more suitable for plates and cups.

Bone china: This is made with powdered bone ash mixed with ball clay and kaolin, in a process developed by Josiah Spode and his son, also called Josiah, in the nineteenth century. Again, the kiln temperature is not as high as that used in making porcelain.

Pottery: A catch-all term that usually refers to functional clay objects.

Earthenware: This term applies to the earliest pottery found, usually made from red clay and fired at a low temperature, and it is still available today. Earthenware is naturally porous and needs to be glazed before it is water-resistant.

Stoneware: Made from clay feldspar and silica, stoneware is more durable than earthenware and it is also non-porous.

A SELECTION OF KIRSTEN'S STUDIO TOOLS

With vast technical expertise at her disposal, Kirsten has numerous textbook ways of approaching a restoration. But sometimes she goes off grid, for example, using paint stripper rather than steam or a scalpel to take previously glued ceramics apart. To each project she brings a clear eye and fresh judgement, but these are her most frequently used items.

1. **Sharp scalpel:** To remove aged adhesive used in previous restoration work and also to cut back filling material.

2. **Steam cleaner:** To effectively clean items, a steam cleaner is useful because steam doesn't make anything too wet. Preparation is key and that means removing all dirt and dust, not just for aesthetics, but also to ensure the adhesives bond properly. Conservation is a niche area, so Kirsten's steam cleaner, with its narrow nozzle and jet of steam, was in fact made for companies constructing dentures.

3. **Specially manufactured adhesives:** The kind conservators like Kirsten use will stay stable for 50 or even 100 years in the correct conditions, which avoids sagging yellow glue appearing around repairs in the future .

4. **Magic tape:** Used for ceramics repair as it is clear and stretchy.

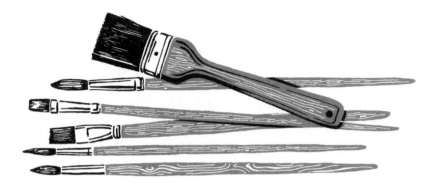

5. **Paint brushes:** These are necessary to complete the decorative pattern that's been disrupted by a breakage. For delicate patterns she uses the finest available.

6. **Specialist water-based acrylics:** She uses these for re-touching. Her aim with artwork is not only accuracy, but also to recreate the tone and ambience, sympathetically blending the restoration to the style of the piece.

7. **Sandpaper and polishing fabrics:** Repairs are made smooth with the use of fine glass paper and cloths.

My Favourite Tools

Kirsten's go-to tool is a flexible steel spatula (size no. 47) that she's used since she was a student. With it she delves into hidden crevices and prods at previous restorations, applies filler to cracks and mixes pigments for painting. At work it's like an extension of her hand. When one breaks, she buys a replacement from a specialist British company established 125 years ago to provide tools for sculptors.

HALLMARKS OF THE ERA

Ceramics have existed alongside mankind since the start of the earliest civilisation, when pliable riverside mud was sun-dried to form plates or vessels.

There's a rich history associated with it but few people today will have a Ming vase, made during the rule of a Chinese dynasty which ended in the mid-seventeenth century, or even a piece of English Delftware, tin glazed pottery made between 1550 and the late eighteenth century. But there is an opportunity here to define some of the major movements that frame ceramic history.

18TH CENTURY

For the enthusiastic amateur a tour of china likely to be found at the back of the cupboard probably starts in the era of Josiah Wedgwood. He went into business in Burslem, Stoke-on-Trent, amid a highly competitive market, and instituted all the principles of industrialisation.

A stickler for high standards, Wedgwood was also fascinated by scientific advances. He is credited with perfecting transfer printing on to pieces, to replace the labourious hand-painting process, as well as pioneering marketing techniques which saw his pottery sold across the globe. One of his great commercial successes was branded 'Queensware' after Queen Charlotte commissioned a tea service in his cream-coloured china in 1765. Afterwards he trumpeted the royal link at every opportunity.

His great rival, Josiah Spode, is credited with advances in transfer printing in underglaze and raising the quality of bone china. Both men dominated the pottery industry that was flourishing in the eighteenth century and more people had the chance to own their own dinner services than ever before.

19TH CENTURY

All the well-defined cultural movements that swept through British society after this point had a marked influence on ceramics. The Arts and Crafts movement, in which William Morris was a leading figure, fell back on simple design, luxuriant glaze and assured quality as a protest against industrialization. It was hotly followed by Art Nouveau, recognizable for its sinuous curves, flowing lines and using nature as its major inspiration.

EARLY 20TH CENTURY

Following the First World War, Art Deco prevailed, with startling geometric shapes, bold colours and innovative design. Clarice Cliff and Susie Cooper were amongst its most famous designers. Then came the decorative modernism of the jazz age.

But it was practicalities that were to make a bigger mark on the ceramics industry in the twentieth century than design. Decoration by coloured lithography first appeared late in then. In short, it's a printing process rooted in the solid chemical principle that grease and water don't mix, thus limiting the absorption of ink, but blips in its results had British potters quickly returning to more conventional options. After the First World War it was still considered expensive despite its extensive use in Europe, but by the 1950s the process dominated, widening the range of decorative pottery.

POST-WAR

Its contribution was especially noticeable as manufacturers responded to the austerity of the war years with richer and more ornate designs.

There were strong colours and a sense of confidence in 1960s design as British style proliferated. Although it didn't last, there were ceramic success stories, including the soaring popularity of Scandanavian design.

It's also worth noting that for every modern pattern there were large numbers of traditional ones throughout the twentieth century that remained family favourites, with Royal Albert's old country roses being prominent among them.

Technological changes in the kitchen called for a new dynamism and saw British designers and producers respond with improved clay and glazes so that pots could tolerate the microwave, a freezer and dishwashers, and could be transferred effortlessly to the dinner table. Despite astonishing progress, crazing, the spider's web of fracture lines that appear when a glaze is under duress, still torments less experienced ceramicists today.

PROJECTS

HOW TO FIX A BROKEN ARM OR HEAD
ON A PORCELAIN FIGURINE

Frequently broken, and hardest to mend, is a plate or platter, when even experts like Kirsten are challenged. When it is created, a plate is charged with an inner tension during manufacture in the kiln. The breakage means that tautness is gone, and recreating it so that the plate properly aligns is problematic. Handles are likewise difficult, with gravity working against repairs in progress. But there are easier tasks to undertake, like attaching an arm or head detached from a figurine.

1. Firstly, thoroughly clean all the pieces involved. Wash and thoroughly air dry them – Kirsten leaves them for several days before starting work.

2. Before starting the repair, wipe exposed edges with acetone to make sure they are grease and grime free.

3. On a clean surface, lay out the bits that are being reassembled to get some idea of how to rebuild and to see if any of the pieces are missing.

4. With some previously cut thin strips of magic tape at hand, do a trial run to establish in which order the pieces should be put in place.

5. Try not to scrape fragments together as that risks losing the sharp connections that exist between pieces.

6. Number the pieces so you know that you won't miss out part of the puzzle.

7. Choose an adhesive that's suitable for the material, ideally one that's softer than the item so any errors are reversible.

8. Don't use too much of it.

9. As you work, use tape again to hold the pieces in place like an extra pair of hands while the adhesive cures.

10. Wipe away excess adhesive with acetone on cotton wool swabs.

11. Stand the item safely while it dries, putting the least pressure possible on the repaired area. If gravity is likely to draw the newly attached limb down, then consider using a sand box to support it while the adhesive cures.

12. Remove the tape when the adhesive is dried, or cured, and remove any further protruding excess with a scalpel.

13. Cracks and small areas of loss can be filled using fine surface Polyfilla. If necessary, rub back carefully using fine sandpaper.

14. Study the item carefully to work out how best to re-touch the repair, if necessary. This can be done with specialist ceramic restoration acrylic glaze and colours. You don't have to necessarily ape the work of the original artist as creating an overall impression may be sufficient.

MEMORABLE MOMENTS

Kirsten Ramsay: 'There is nothing I like more than sitting, cleaning objects. It's an opportunity to look at how they are made. You get to see amazing details that normally would be missed.'

Heirlooms aren't necessarily items of high value or fine art. It's the things that have sentimental significance or longevity that gladden the heart. For one family, its treasured memento was a large, brash barge-wear teapot passed down through the female line, representing the contribution of generations past and the hopes that lay wrapped up in those yet to come.

Sadly, the passage of the teapot was going to be interrupted after the untimely death of a 28-year-old mum. It meant the next recipient would be her 16-month-old daughter and her grandparents were determined the youngster should receive it in the best possible shape.

Barge-wear is distinctive for its chocolate brown glaze, usually described as treacle, and its bulging hand colour motifs. It was made in and around Burton-on-Trent between about 1860 until 1914 and often bought as a gift to mark a birth, anniversary or a marriage. Sometimes the banner on the side of barge-wear has a less personal motto, like 'Remember Me'. Commonly called Measham china, it was named for a town lying on the Ashby canal where the pottery was sold.

This time Kirsten was presented with something that had a number of cracks and chips – but those were not her biggest challenge. Missing from the top of the lid was a finial in the shape of a tiny teapot that had to be made from scratch.

Still, her first priority was to consolidate a crack running down the side of the teapot which rendered the pear-shaped body at risk of breaking into fragments. When that was done she put a putty base on the lid where the new teapot finial would be attached.

Then it was time to hand-sculpt the new baby teapot that mimicked the larger model, in pliable clay. Having mirrored the details on the body of the Victorian pot, she let the new addition dry, rubbed it down and finally painted it in a treacly brown, carefully manoeuvring the teapot lid from workbench to teapot by holding its base.

Finally, it was in pristine condition and ready for the family to collect, hoping to one day tell the story of a mother's love through an item lovingly maintained.

* * *

Gifts personalised by a photograph have always been popular – although decades ago they were not as ubiquitous as today.

When one Irishman brought a soft heart-shaped china plate bearing a hand-coloured picture of his wife, it became a symbol of enduring love. It accompanied them when they emigrated to London and took pride of place in the family home for years.

But while marriage and family life stayed strong, the plate was altogether less resilient. At one point it was accidentally shattered and no amount of glue could disguise the damage.

Five weeks after the woman in the photo died, it was brought into The Repair Shop by her daughter, now more attached to the cracked keepsake than ever before.

For Kirsten it was a daunting task, with fractures clearly evident across the transposed photograph and bits of the decorative plate edge missing. Her first job was to thoroughly clean it and remove the adhesive built up around the well-meaning repairs that had already taken place. She paid special attention to the break edges to ensure they were free of old glue and grime.

In a dry run, before fixing the plate, she put the shards together using her fingertips to sense a bite, which happens when broken edges properly lock into place. While most did, there was one section that didn't produce that connection she expected. For a second time she cleaned the edges and came across a scintilla of old adhesive that had been missed. When all the pieces were bonded into place the plate once again regained some of the structural strength it would have had as new.

To recreate the missing decoration surrounding the plate she pressed moulding material firmly into some that remained intact. She then moved this newly created mould to the missing section and filled it with epoxy resin, forming a new frill. Although the plate and the new section were both white, Kirsten knew from years of experience that not all whites are equal. So when the resin was dry she had to carefully colour match the paint, adding minute amounts of different hues to get the right result.

The last stage was the most difficult, to disguise the repaired lines that seared across the photograph. Dark colours would have left the picture looking sinister so Kirsten chose minimal intervention that would nonetheless mask the intrusive lines. For a grieving daughter, it was a poignant reminder of a woman who remained at the heart of her family.

* * *

There are a lucky few that do possess work by acknowledged artists, although that didn't end well for one woman whose stunning terracotta jug made by Frenchman Jean Lurçat ended up in pieces on her floor. It danced off the window sill thanks to heavy duty drilling going on in the road outside.

Born in 1892, Lurcat studied alongside Matisse, Cezanne and Renoir. He is best remembered for exquisite tapestries – as well as his work for the French Resistance during the Second World War. This jug was reminiscent of the ceramics produced by Picasso, who Lurcat also knew.

The base of the white jug with a bold black design was largely unscathed but its top section and handle were shattered. The owner scooped up all the fragments, even brushing its dust into an envelope – a move that Kirsten advocates for all breakages. At her workbench Kirsten then laid all the pieces, from large chunks to slithers, as she tried to work out where each belonged.

Even the smallest shred was replaced where possible, to reduce the amount of time spent filling, sanding and re-painting. Still, it didn't look like a new model based on the original, as some of the scars still showed.

It was, said Kirsten, a sympathetic restoration, meaning that it wasn't perfect but nor was the integrity of the item substantially altered. When the three-dimensional puzzle was completed she decided not to smother it in paint to disguise the repair lines but leave them visible although not eye-catchingly apparent. The jug's unexpected fall – and ensuing repair – had been absorbed into its story.

USEFUL TERMS

Adhesive: The conservator's term for glue.

Bond: The conservator's term for sticking.

Abrade: To wear away by friction.

Sprung: A tension introduced in production into bowls, platters and big dishes and released when it's broken.

Shards: Pieces of broken ceramic.

Sherds: Fragments of historic pottery, also called potsherd.

On glaze: Decoration on top of the glaze, like gilding.

Underglaze: Decoration beneath the glaze, like painting.

Micro-mesh: A mildly abrasive fabric, which helps to smooth down ceramic surfaces after repairs or prior to polishing.

Plastic polish: Originally designed for cleaning the canopies of Spitfires and still used to clean aircraft windscreens today, plastic polish is used in ceramics restoration to add shine.

Renaissance wax: Developed by the British Museum in the fifties, this is another way of providing a protective coat to some items.

Kirsten's List of Do's and Don'ts

- *Do clean decorative ceramics if they are not broken. The first step is to determine whether the item is glazed, that is, whether its surface has a glass-like coating. This is protective, so it's fine to wash ceramics in a washing-up bowl with mild, soapy water. But don't treat broken or unglazed items the same way as this can lead to damage and staining.*

- *Don't use superglue in a ceramics repair. Ideally, it should be possible to take a repaired item apart again at some point, particularly if the glue has aged and discoloured.*

- *Do try the tap test to work out if your item has unseen cracks. Using your knuckle, gently knock its body and listen. There's a ringing sound if it's intact, but if a dull thud sounds, it means there's a flaw to be found.*

- *Don't be tempted to fix a handle on a teacup in case the repair gives way and you end up with hot liquid in your lap. Only mend it if it's to become a decorative item.*

PAINTINGS

When his favourite painting was holed during a house move, Terry Courtley considered mending it with a patch and some paints. It's a quick-fix, low-cost solution that no doubt lures many into the treacherous territory of DIY art repairs, blind to the pitfalls.

Fortunately he decided against this initial instinct and brought it instead to The Repair Shop so conservator Lucia Scalisi could unleash her expertise – and reveal just what it takes to patch up a painting so you can't see the joins.

As a young man who had just started a small business, Terry bought the painting having been attracted by the tree-lined avenue depicted in it. He had grown up on the south coast and, with its oak trees and parkland, the picture reminded him of the Ilex Way at Goring-by-Sea in West Sussex.

In the bottom left-hand corner was the monogram JWM and a date, 1887. Not only did it now have a gap in the canvas, its finer detail was obscured by years of gathered dust. Altogether, it was a complex repair of a canvas made brittle by age.

Lucia's first task was cleaning the tabby weave canvas, a satisfying if slow process. At the start of it she carried out a 'spit' cleaning test, with saliva-soaked cotton wool rolled gently over a small section of the canvas. Enzymes in the saliva help to remove the loose surface dirt and give telling results. An oily film reveals the picture has likely been hung in a city, yellow brown marks indicate it belonged to a smoker, waxy residues probably point to a church setting where candles have frequently been lit, while smoke ash signposts that it's fire-affected. No one has enough spit to tackle a major item, so surface cleaning is carried out with a solution tailor-made for each task.

Lucia can discern as much from the wall-facing back of a painting as the front. Flipped over, she sees how well it fits the frame and whether it's previously been lined or cut down. She may well catch a glimpse of a hitherto hidden corner that will reveal how just dirty it has become.

When she lifted this 130-year-old painting out of its frame she was greeted with the expected level of dust and fly carcasses – previously she has found the skeleton of a bird tucked away here. Even glass-covered paintings can become grime traps if the paper on the back is torn. This time the detritus was swiftly dealt with by her professional museum vacuum, specifically made for delicate objects. Carefully, she removed the tacks that attached the painting to its wooden stretcher.

At the margins of the painting there was ample canvas to snip out a small section that would patch the holes. The next job was to line the back of the canvas, to give it additional strength and stability and to hold these sections of infilling firmly in place.

She rolled out a heat-seal adhesive film on the back of the canvas and then pressed on to it some polyester sail cloth, using a specially made iron set at a specific temperature to activate the bonding process. Although the nap bond that she created was strong it was also reversible so, if it was heated again, the sail cloth could have been removed.

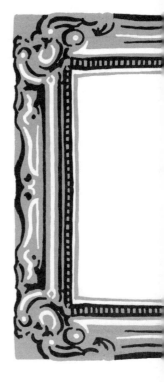

After cutting away the excess lining fabric she placed the painting back on its stretcher, using original tack holes to avoid making extra perforations, and precisely folded the corners as if she was making a hospital bed. Looked at from the front the surface was now uneven, dipping where the patches had been laid, so she used filler to raise the level, 'Like plastering on a micro-scale,' she explained. When all exposed areas of canvas were covered and smooth, Lucia could finally open her box of paints.

Oil paints are not an option in any of Lucia's projects. The drying process takes months and by the end of it, the colours have changed from the original.

Lucia works with dry pigments that she mixes with a medium. She not only has to match the colours, but she must emulate the techniques used by this unknown artist to blend her modern brushstrokes with those applied during the nineteenth century. The meticulous work paid off, however, as when Terry came to collect his painting it looked pristine once more.

PIGMENTS AND PAINT

In simple terms, paint is two materials mixed together: a pigment – which used alone won't stay where it's put – and a medium to bind it so it becomes serviceable. In Lucia's studio dry pigments are stored in glass jars, while the medium she uses is a synthetic resin, chosen for its robust anti-ageing quality.

It's not the only option, though, as numerous mediums can be used with pigments, including glue, casein, waxes, clay and oils. Painters then need a diluent – solvents for synthetic resin, for example, and turpentine for oils – to make the colour flow from the brush.

Earth pigments are long-held palette staples, but that's not to say that there haven't been some changes to the colours used by present-day artists. Lead white was present in most paintings – and household paint – until the twentieth century, when its toxic qualities were finally acknowledged. Titanium white is today's safe alternative.

As well as the six earth pigments Lucia uses daily, there are organic pigments from plants and chemistry set colours too, comprising a palette of 15 dependable colours that she can blend to produce many more. Although the pigments are costly, she uses only tiny amounts with each project, decanting them individually into small glass vials to contain colour pollution.

Conservators are few in number and must pass a colour blindness test before qualifying. With colour blindness affecting an estimated one in 12 men, as compared to one in 200 women, it means there are a more limited number of male candidates for a world where discerning minutely different shades is a prerequisite for the job.

A Selection of Lucia's Workshop Tools

Lucia needs a surprisingly limited selection of tools to salvage or save art of the past.

1. **Fine blade scalpel:** A scalpel like this is usually used for surgery and she is as cautious as any doctor when she wields it on a canvas.

2. **Easel:** The ratchet-operated double easel at her London studio once belonged to Victorian painter George Watts.

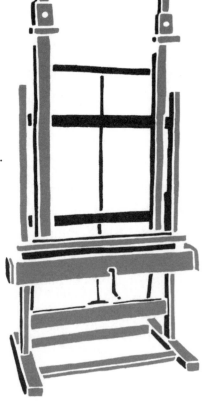

3. **Table:** Lucia needs an uncluttered horizontal space to investigate paintings.

4. **Paint brushes:** Lucia uses expertly made brushes that control the flow of paint.

5. **Heated spatula:** This is used for re-attaching paint flakes.

6. **Lining iron:** This iron secures new canvas to the back of an historic painting.

7. **Cotton wool and bamboo sticks:** These are used to make cleaning swabs.

8. **Chemicals:** As part of more heavy-duty cleaning processes or to remove obstinate layers of varnish, Lucia uses a range of chemicals that she needs a licence to buy.

My Favourite Tools

Conservators like Lucia must borrow from other professions to assemble their equipment. As a consequence, her favourite tool is one usually used in dentistry to mix fillings. She bought two as a student from a dentists' practice, but only uses one, which nestles comfortably in the crook of her hand.

How to Wrap Paintings for Transport

For years Lucia worked at the Victoria and Albert Museum in London, helping to maintain a vast art collection. When it comes to moving pictures, institutions use tailor-made packing cases lined with Plastazote, inert foam that will safely cradle precious cargo until it reaches its destination. Then it's left for days to acclimatise in new surroundings before being opened. That's not an option available to most of us, but there's plenty of scope for paintings to be damaged in transit, as Terry has illustrated. Here Lucia advises on the best way to package pictures.

1. First protect the vulnerable corners by taking a sheet of acid-free tissue paper and folding it into a chunky strip.

2. About two-thirds of the way along, fold the strip 90 degrees, creating a thick right-angled triangle at its heart, compared to two thinner end pieces, which all together look like a pair of wings.

3. Put the midpoint of the triangle's longest edge diagonally across the face of the picture so it touches one corner.

4. Fold both edges of the strip behind the picture so a well-fitting pointed cap is created.

5. Fix in place, using masking tape rather than Sellotape.

6. Make a similar tissue paper cap for the other three corners.

7. Repeat the steps above using bubble wrap to consolidate protection.

8. Take two lengths of cotton tape, one to encircle the height and the second the width of the picture. Lay them across the front of the picture and tape the ends to the back of the picture if it is covered. Tie them if not.

9. After that, the paining is ready to be wrapped in tissue paper and, for a limited time, in bubble wrap to add further protection.

MEMORABLE MOMENTS

Lucia: 'Everything we do there is a story to it in one way or the other. I just love this workshop because of that.'

Children playing hide-and-seek at home sank gratefully into an obscured spot beneath a desk and behind a painting being stored on the floor during house decoration. Naturally, they wanted to gain an advantage on the seeker so they used a pencil to poke several spy-holes through the canvas that blocked them from view.

At the time they didn't realise the painting, done by a distant family member, was worth thousands of pounds. Worse still, when art conservator Lucia saw it she not only recognised it as the work of Fred Appleyard (1874–1963), whose paintings hang in the Tate art gallery today, but suspected the damage might be beyond repair.

The owner – the artist was his grandmother's uncle – wasn't surprised to hear her sober verdict, given the extent of the holes and the tears that now peppered the country cottage scene.

Lucia's first challenge was to release the canvas from its frame. Immediately she passed the wooden surround to Will to enlarge its window by 4mm on each side, so the picture could be replaced rather than rammed in after the repair.

As always, her overarching aim was to keep the artwork as close to its original condition as possible. For this she has an array of specialist equipment and professional techniques that would leave even the most enthusiastic amateur floundering.

Aiming to preserve as much of the existing paint as possible she fixed the perforated edges around the rips using tape, so nothing more could flake off and be lost. When that was in place she flipped the painting over to work on the back of the canvas, initially using a process of carefully applied moisture in minute quantities and blotting paper to shrink the stretched fibres back to something like their proper length before placing nylon gossamer patches over the holes.

Back on the front side she carefully filled the crevices left by the healed rips using an acrylic filler, that was both soft and plasticised. This has to be gently smoothed to make an even surface before the paint can be applied. Then it was a case not only of colour matching but of being faithful to the integrity of the artist. The reward for patient hours spent poring over the artwork was that Lucia exceeded her own expectations, producing a canvas where outward signs of her work were all-but invisible.

* * *

At the start of the twentieth century living in a rambling country home with extensive gardens wasn't solely the preserve of the rich.

There were staff who kept the house in order and gardeners who saw to the luxuriant plot surrounding it.

During the Second World War a housekeeper ended up living at Ickneild House in Tring, Hertfordshire, with her daughter and granddaughter, a young girl who spent her courting days in the garden of the house and finally left there as a bride.

Today one of her prized possessions is a canvas of that same house painted by its owner, Violet Mcdougall, in the early part of the twentieth century and presented to her grandmother. Unfortunately, it was extensively damaged by fire 40 years ago and had been stowed in the attic since.

Some of its problems were starkly apparent, like a broken frame and substantial white marks where the paint had been burnt. Only on closer inspection did Lucia notice a vast array of small spots that were tiny but deep so would catch the light if they were left untended.

But her first task was to consolidate the lumps of paint that were in danger of lifting, using a heated spatula to activate adhesive which were in turn sealed by small sections of acid-free tissue paper. Then it was time to carefully clean the canvas, removing the tissue as she progressed. Beneath there were blazes of bright colour along flower beds that had been dulled by accrued dirt.

Lucia then had to fill an estimated one thousand spots of paint loss, ranging from small to minute, to ensure every semblance of damage was eradicated. To do this she put on an illuminated magnifying head-band, so she could see almost every original brush stroke. For Lucia, getting as close to a work of art as the creator is one of the privileges of the her job as conservator.

Using colour-matched tones she finally covered the filler she'd put on without having to encroach on the artist's work. The aim was that no one would be to see her contribution while the vast majority of the original paint was still intact.

For the owners the revived painting, now a sentimental symbol of a love story that lasted a lifetime, made them feel young once more.

USEFUL TERMS

Stretcher: The wooden framework around which a painting is mounted.

Diluent: A substance that dilutes.

Winchester bottles: Narrow-necked 2.5 litre glass bottles that contain the costly chemicals Lucia uses in her work.

Tabby weave: Also known as plain weave, this is the most commonly occurring canvas with a warp and weft threads simply interwoven.

Polyurethene varnish: A mid-twentieth century invention that's particularly difficult to remove from paintings because it's insoluble and goes grey with age.

Lucia's List of Do's and Don'ts

Lucia's love of art was sparked when she was a schoolgirl, and fanned by Sheffield's museum service picture lending scheme. Having been loaned a picture, she took it home on the bus, which would probably be top on her list of 'don'ts' today. Here's her guide to best domestic practice when it comes to art.

- *Do hang pictures on the wall. It's the safest place for them to be.*

- *Don't touch the surface of a painting.*

- *Don't wipe the frame or any other part of the picture with a wet cloth. If you don't clean a painting, it probably won't fall apart, but should you wash it, it might.*

- *Don't used bubble wrap as a long-term solution for storing pictures. It releases a gas that may harm the picture and could also pockmark its surface.*

CLOCKS

Effortlessly, an assortment of cogs and wheels spinning this way and that ensures the hands of a mechanical clock move forwards and at the right frequency. Skeleton clocks, so called for having no body, are enchanting showpieces for revealing the exquisite harmony of every tiny motion. First seen in France at the end of the eighteenth century, the popularity of English-made ones chimed with a Gothic revival in Victorian times and modern versions are still sought after today.

Nigel and Viv Burge had inherited a prized skeleton clock, which once belonged to Nigel's soldier grandfather. After a First World War shell rendered his left arm useless, he took up running to keep fit and won the clock in an athletics competition. The tone of its tick was a cherished childhood memory for Nigel.

Still in pride of place on the mantelpiece, the clock had in truth become neither used nor ornament, as it looked jaded and no longer worked.

Poignantly, the couple brought the clock to The Repair Shop after their son Peter also suffered a catastrophic injury to his left arm following a motorcycle accident. He too had his sights set on competition, for him the Tokyo Paralympics, and they hoped the clock could once again be a shining symbol of courage in adversity.

Clock restorer Steve Fletcher was bowled over by it, not least because the original glass dome that shielded the clock from dust and damage was still intact. His first job was to dismantle the scores of parts, large and small, and to carry out his first, but by no means his only, assessment of what had gone wrong.

Embarking on every project Steve is filled with anticipation, not knowing what he might find. Although decades separate himself and the manufacturer, he feels an affinity as they are treading the same path. In this case the original craftsman was Charles Wieland, one of 35 clockmakers listed in Norwich in 1854.

Almost immediately Steve discovered major problems. One of the pivots responsible for bearing a main wheel was worn to almost nothing, while another cog had a section of teeth bent over so badly they were no longer capable of the slick operation working clocks require.

The pivot was beyond redemption, but forging its replacement was an especially tricky task. In substituting new for old he snipped off the damaged pivot end, drilled the rest out and forged a replacement using specialist equipment. Then he reached for a broken watch-repairers' tool that he'd kept for the useful size of its blunt and tapered blade. Clasping it firmly in one hand, with the damaged cog in the other, he set about manually levering back the bent teeth to an upright position.

Steve transformed the tarnished cogs and wheels by dipping each one into ammonia-based clock cleaning fluid and then scrubbing them with various brushes, so they appeared as new. But this was a project he could not finish alone. This skeleton clock was mounted on a rosewood base decorated with an inlaid metal pattern – and both were in dire need of refurbishment. Happily, The Repair Shop experts are always keen to work as a team.

Will Kirk, the woodwork expert, replaced missing veneer with a matching grain. The new patch was lighter than the rest, but he used pigment and polish to conceal that. As he by turns polished and sanded the base to bring out a long-lost lustre, silversmith Brenton West recreated the intricate metal inlay. Having photocopied the original, Brenton painstakingly cut out a pattern from the paper picture, stuck it on a piece of brass and sawed out a replica.

Then Steve was ready to re-assemble the clock and its many components. Blessed with a brain that sees things in three dimensions and with years of experience behind him, he deftly orchestrated its reconstruction. Sometimes, despite his best efforts, a repaired clock fails to work and he's always prepared to start from scratch, carrying out more assessments as he goes on to find any obscure problem he has missed. This time, however, the mechanism settled back into working life immediately. After the glass was cleaned and a replacement red braid was put on to mask the seam between dome and clock base, it was ready for collection by the Burges. For Nigel it was an emotional moment, made more so when he immediately presented the clock to son Peter.

SERVICING A CLOCK

A ticking clock marks the daily rhythm of a household, with everyone growing accustomed to its calm heartbeat. But there's a risk people take this soothing sound for granted. Inside, the movement of a clock may beat tens of millions of times a year. During a lifetime, the number runs into the billions.

So, it probably shouldn't be a surprise to know that clocks, both large and small, need regular servicing. When owners neglect to put a care plan in place for their timepiece, they put its longevity at risk.

The aim is not just to keep the innards of the clock clean and shiny, but to preserve them by reducing wear and tear. For the purposes of both conservation and maintaining value, it's preferable, but not always possible, to rejuvenate existing parts.

Small clocks need more regular servicing, with carriage clocks benefitting from an overhaul about every eight years. Every dozen years a grandfather clock needs attention. Most clocks run for eight days after being wound and if they begin to falter on that timescale, it's probably a sign they are in need of a service.

In between times, clocks may well need lubrication to keep their movements silky smooth. Without oil, a clock – like a car – may well seize up.

Although this is basic maintenance, both are jobs for an expert clockmaker as tinkering with the inner workings has all kinds of pitfalls, according to Steve. It's essential, for example, to put oil only into the correct places. And it's a specialist clock oil that's called for, rather than multipurpose varieties. Steve's attended to numerous clocks that have come to a shuddering halt after being subjected to a lubricating spray, usually one that gets its best results on car engines.

Clockwork Toys

With his mechanical dexterity, Steve can turn his talents not only to clocks, but also to clockwork toys.

Although Leonardo da Vinci is credited with making a clockwork toy in the early sixteenth century, a golden age occured three centuries after that, when moving tin toys were in vogue. At The Repair Shop, Steve fixed a wind-up Alfa Romeo toy racing car, dating from 1925, repairing its rack and pinion steering system as well as its internal mechanism. The decline in the popularity of mechanical toys corresponds with a rise in the number of battery-powered toys at the end of the twentieth century.

With all their internal joints rivetted into place, clockwork toys were not made to be repaired and, once again, it's unlikely an inexperienced hand or eye could successfully overhaul one. It means breaking into the clockwork mechanism's housing, so there are two repairs to be done instead of one.

A Selection of Steve's Clockmaker Tools

Like most craftsmen, the walls of Steve's workshop are lined with tools, typically with the fine proportions necessary for working with the small parts of a clock. If he doesn't have the right tool for the job, he's likely to design and make one.

1. **Screwdrivers:** Steve bought his first screwdriver when he was aged ten. Since then, his collection has expanded somewhat. In addition to using a screwdriver belonging to his grandfather, Steve inherited tools from his father, also a clock and watch repairer.

2. **Pliers:** Steve has in excess of 50 pliers, each designed slightly differently and appropriate for job-specific tasks.

3. **Tweezers:** These are used for picking up and locating the small parts of clocks and watches.

4. **Lathe:** This is used for a multitude of tasks, for example, turning a new pivot for a clock.

5. **Glasses:** Steve is often filmed wearing two or even three glasses at the same time, to get the maximum magnification necessary for the job in hand.

My Favourite Tools

Steve's favourite tool is a 6 inch (15cm) long ratchet screwdriver, with the shiny maroon of its handle now mostly worn down to wood, hinting at its great age. It's something that belonged to his grandfather, Fred, also a clock and watch repairer. After Fred joined the army in the First World War and was dispatched to the Middle East, his skills were spotted by an officer who sent him back to the comparative safety of the support lines to mend watches and military instruments. As a consequence, he survived the conflict and came home to Witney in Oxfordshire to resume his trade.

It's not known when Fred bought this screwdriver, but in his later years he used it every day, even after his retirement in 1964. After Steve set up a workshop, Fred was a daily visitor and dispensed plenty of advice. Steve was keen to plot his own path, but down the years he has discovered the wisdom of his grandfather's words – and also found he inherited the older man's infinite patience. Now when Steve wields the screwdriver, he feels as if he is holding hands with Fred across the decades. Fortunately, the balance of the tool and the quality of its blade have not been diminished by the passing years.

MEMORABLE MOMENTS

Steve: 'It really gives me great satisfaction to take a clock or watch that is important to somebody and keep it alive for future generations. It is a passion.'

To clockmaker Steve all timepieces are things of beauty. Yet even after years in the business he sometimes encounters examples that even to his experienced eye are little short of stunning. One Victorian clock brought into The Repair Shop captivated him for its sturdy mechanism and eye-catching decoration.

The clock was built in extravagant Louis XIV style, with its pendulum in the shape of the sun. But it was the case with its breath-taking brass and tortoiseshell inlayed patterns that elevated this model above some others of a similar age.

Called Boulle work, the marquetry technique was named for its pioneer, Frenchman Andre-Charles Boulle, who came to prominence when Louis XIV was on the French throne. During the era an obsession for ornate design spread across the continent, not least because Louis XIV, known as 'the Sun King', suddenly withdrew freedom of worship in France, forcing 200,000 Protestant Huguenots to leave for Holland and Britain, many of them accomplished craftsmen.

Steve immediately identified the clock in hand as a Victorian replica built with outstanding craftsmanship. The job naturally fell into two distinct parts: the clock mechanism and the case.

Once it was unscrewed and removed from its housing the heavy clock mechanism was taken to pieces. As he examined each component, Steve found one bent tooth on a single cog capable of seizing up the strike mechanism. All the parts were cleaned before then being re-built by Steve with gloved hands, so there was no risk of human sweat tarnishing the brass workings.

With the case empty he used cotton wool charged with brass cleaning fluid to rejuvenate the Boulle work. That in turn left the mounts decorating the clock face looking dull so these were duly dipped in clock cleaning fluid so they matched the gleam on the rest of the clock. To complete it, he coated both with a Shellac-based lacquer to lock in the glossy finish.

When the two elements of the clock were re-united it was time to see if the chime was sounding sweetly. In fact, it was dull and echoed, until Steve adjusted the gong block. After that it was back in tune and sounded every bit as splendid as it now appeared.

* * *

An elderly 'grandfather' clock arrived for a check-up at The Repair Shop in the nick of time. Although problems weren't evident at first glance, it was dangerously wobbly on its feet. On closer investigation, Steve and woodwork expert Will discovered the wooden plinth at the base of the clock had been made so brittle with the dryness of age it had broken. The elegant timepiece, which towered above them both, was close to toppling over.

Although an engraved plaque on the clock face dated it to 1712 Steve estimated it was probably made in about 1750. The maker

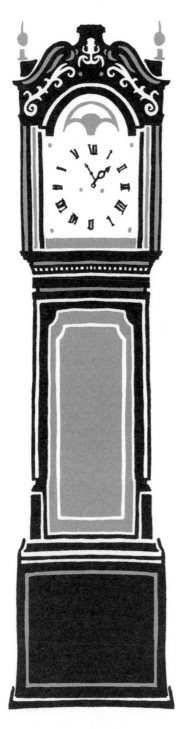

was William Robb, a long-case clock specialist mostly based in Montrose, Scotland, who produced handsome French-style specimens throughout the last half of the eighteenth century.

Even Will didn't realise the extent of the problem when he first inspected the clock case, marking missing corners and other areas scheduled for repair with small swabs of blue tape. Only when the mechanism was removed and he could heave the wooden case on to a work bench did the age-related problems fully reveal themselves. He set about bonding together wood that had sheared off and nourishing the upright panels to re-create a stable case.

Steve had problems of his own to contend with, as the workings of the clock were black with age. It had been at least 20 years since it last worked and, prior to that, Steve estimated it had ticked some seven and a half billion times in its life before its enforced retirement.

Unsurprisingly, some components were worn, although he managed to made minute critical adjustments with careful use of a scalpel rather than having to find replacement parts. There was one new introduction, though: a hammer that would sound the chime every hour.

When it arrived, the ornately engraved clock face was entirely brass. However, originally it would have had a silver-coloured centre and it seemed appropriate to mimic that oft-seen style. Steve worked silver powder gently into this section to give the clock a face lift that would make it look the same as it did in its youth and complete its transformation from a jaded and distant echo of former glory into a show-stopper for a semi.

* * *

A broken pocket watch was the sole link for one Dutchman to his family's history. Given its traumatic journey, it was fortunate to survive at all.

His grandparents lived in Indonesia when they were forced to flee in the face of the Japanese invasion in 1942. Leaving all their possessions, his grandmother only had time to save the watch, which had an Albert chain and a fob bearing her photo.

The couple were separated, with his grandfather sent to work on the Burma railway while his grandmother was dispatched to a camp in Sumatra. As soon as she could, she stitched the watch into the hem of her dress, hiding it from not only guards but other hungry prisoners who would have traded it for food.

Happily both survived the war and returned home to Holland with the watch, their only possession from the era and a symbol of their courage in adversity. But the watch, a Swiss-made Invicta model, hadn't worked for decades before arriving at The Repair Shop.

The moving story resonated with Steve who, after inspecting it with a magnifying eyeglass, was hopeful it would be back ticking after a rigorous clean. But this wasn't something that could be carried out beneath the thatched roof of The Repair Shop barn. He removed it to a more sterile atmosphere as the workings were so fine that any descending dust would only add to the issue.

Both hour and minute hands needs straightening and an additional one had to be found to mark the seconds, which recorded on a small dial on the watch face. A specialist dial restorer helped Steve clean the face and restore the delicately drawn roman numerals on it.

After it was put back together, the watch began to work once more, proving Steve's theory that prison camp grime was the cause of its problems. As the watch once gave reassurance to a hungry internee, its restoration was a comfort to her surviving relatives.

USEFUL TERMS

Movement: The clock's mechanism.

Clock gears: These make the hands of the clock work, comprising larger wheels and smaller pinions.

Balance wheel: A weighted wheel that rotates back and forth to regulate time.

Pendulum: Another method of regulating the speeds at which a clock will run.

Escapement: The mechanical link that releases the power to a balance wheel or pendulum.

Mainspring: The power source for mechanical clocks and watches, with energy stored in it after being wound.

Hairspring: This controls the running speed for a clock or watch with a balance wheel.

Weights: Another power source for differently designed clocks.

Stoppers: A term used by Steve's grandfather Fred and other clockmakers to describe clocks that have an intermittent problem. Despite a repairer's best efforts, they can randomly stop, causing frustration for craftsman and customer alike.

Steve's List of Do's and Don'ts

Stripping down a clock or watch is not for the faint-hearted. There are many parts inside a clock: they may be tiny, fragile and/or have three or four different functions. Ambition is all very well, but without previous experience, there's a risk the components will end up as so much scrap on the workbench. But still, there is much you can do to help preserve the life of your clock.

- *Don't put a clock on the mantelpiece of a working fire, or above or near a radiator. The heat will adversely affect its mechanism. Keep it out of direct sunlight too, for the same reason.*

- *Do make sure your clock is level and stable, whether it's on four feet or hung on a wall, to aid its internal balance. Grandfather clocks – properly called longcase clocks – should stand squarely on the floor or be attached at the back to the wall, to stop the case rocking in sympathy with the pendulum.*

- *Don't carry a clock with its pendulum still attached as that may damage its suspension or skew the clock's balance. Unhook it from the clock casing and carefully lift it out.*

- *Do use a soft cloth or fine paint brush to clean clock cases.*

- *Don't use liquid polish on brass cases in case it seeps into the mechanism.*

- *Do use wax polish rather than silicone sprays when attending to wooden clock cases, to feed the wood.*

- *Don't leave a pendulum clock ticking when you go away. If you let it run down, there's a chance of throwing the clock out of whack or damaging its internal ticker. Stop the pendulum by holding it still for a moment and re-start it when you return.*

- *Do wind a clock fully, but don't try to force those last few clicks of rotation in the hope it will run for longer, as that risks snapping the mainspring.*

- *Don't push clock hands backwards when setting the time. Guide them gently forward around the clock face, pausing if necessary for the clock to strike each hour and half hour.*

- *Do seek advice from a clockmaker about the care of your clock and its internal workings. After the fifteenth century, when weight and spring-driven clocks became increasingly abundant, clocks have been made in all shapes and sizes with different refinements inside, so it's specialist knowledge accrued over years that's needed rather than raw enthusiasm.*

With special thanks to *The Repair Shop* experts
for their contributions to this book.

10

BBC Books, an imprint of Ebury Publishing
20 Vauxhall Bridge Road,
London SW1V 2SA

BBC Books is part of the Penguin Random House group of companies
whose addresses can be found at global.penguinrandomhouse.com

Penguin
Random House
UK

Copyright © Woodland Books 2019

Main text by Karen Farrington

This book is published to accompany the television series entitled
The Repair Shop, first broadcast on BBC Two in 2017

First published by BBC Books in 2019

www.penguin.co.uk

A CIP catalogue record for this book is available from the British Library

ISBN 9781785944604

Printed and bound in Great Britain by Clays Ltd, Elcograf S.p.A.

Penguin Random House is committed to a sustainable future for
our business, our readers and our planet. This book is made
from Forest Stewardship Council® certified paper.

Please behave sensibly and take care when following the step-by-step
guides in this book. The author and publishers disclaim, as far as the
law allows, any liability arising directly or indirectly from the use,
or misuse, of the information contained in this book.